TALES FROM THE MESS

TALES
FROM THE MESS
A MILITARY MISCELLANY

MILES NOONAN

HUTCHINSON
London Melbourne Sydney Auckland Johannesburg

Hutchinson & Co. (Publishers) Ltd

An imprint of the Hutchinson Publishing Group

17–21 Conway Street, London W1P 6JD

Hutchinson Group (Australia) Pty Ltd
30–32 Cremorne Street, Richmond South, Victoria 3121
PO Box 151, Broadway, New South Wales 2007

Hutchinson Group (NZ) Ltd
32–34 View Road, PO Box 40–086, Glenfield, Auckland 10

Hutchinson Group (SA) Pty Ltd
PO Box 337, Bergvlei 2012, South Africa

First published 1983

© Miles Noonan 1983

Set in VIP Baskerville by D. P. Media Limited,
Hitchin, Hertfordshire

Printed and bound in Great Britain
by Anchor Brendon Limited

ISBN 0 09 154460 2

Illustrations from *Punch*, with the exception of those on page 35 from *Bystanders
Fragments from France* by Bruce Bairnsfather; page 40 from the Courtauld Institute
and page 176 from *Soldier Magazine*

CONTENTS

FOREWORD

Before too many querulous old-timers try to prove that Blair Mayne of the SAS could not have been in Cairo on St Patrick's Day in 1941, or that the innovative veterinary experiment in the horse lines of the RHA was in Ahmednagar in 1904 and not in Umballa in 1898, or that an element of doubt hangs about anything else, I should define the principle that has governed the choice of pieces for this collection.

The rule has been that to qualify for inclusion something described must have been *said* to have happened. Whether it did actually happen is no business of mine. It is, in any case, no longer possible to verify many of the entries. So far as the laying of responsibility for accuracy goes, this lets me out.

Some names quoted are genuine. Others have been altered to mitigate possible embarrassment.

I am indebted to a host of volunteer contributors for source material. More often than not they were holding a glass in their hands while they drew on their memories or their versions of other people's memories. Any errors are theirs.

PRO PATRIA

The inscription on a headstone in a Christian
cemetery in India reads:

SACRED TO THE MEMORY OF
CAPTAIN MAURICE JAMES BUTLER,
ROYAL IRISH RIFLES.
ACCIDENTALLY SHOT DEAD BY HIS
BATMAN ON THE FOURTH DAY OF
APRIL, 1882.
'WELL DONE, THOU GOOD AND
FAITHFUL SERVANT'

A SENSE OF RESPONSIBILITY

IT was put to General Sir Douglas Haig, Commander in Chief of the British Expeditionary Force in France in 1916, that it might be no bad thing if he unbent a little from time to time and exchanged a few brief, friendly words with some of the soldiers he commanded. Among the volunteers of the new citizen army were some quite well-educated chaps who might appreciate that sort of thing. There was no question, of course, of suggesting overfamiliarity: just occasional expressions of encouragement, sometimes perhaps even affability.

General Haig, invincibly taciturn and not noted for bonhomie, gave no sign of having registered this revolutionary advice. But it was thought that he must have given it consideration because shortly afterwards he put it into effect.

The individual he chose for his first little chat was selected arbitrarily. He was an isolated operator who was shovelling mud from a roadside ditch. The general spotted him from his staff car. He told the driver to stop and got out. The driver held open the rear door and saluted. The ditch-clearer gaped.

An immaculate figure with a white moustache, a red face that matched the red band around his cap, a colourful splash of medal ribbons and gleaming field boots advanced gloomily upon the ditch.

The general stopped, stared fixedly at the ditcher, and mentally ran through a few possible conversational openings. The soldier stared back, wondering what he had done wrong.

The general finally selected a good one. 'Where did you start the war?' he grunted menacingly.

'I did *not* start the war,' said the soldier defensively.

MILITARY EDUCATION

General: 'MR DE BRIDOON, WHAT IS THE GENERAL USE OF CAVALRY IN MODERN WARFARE?'

Mr de Bridoon: 'WELL, I SUPPOSE TO GIVE TONE TO WHAT WOULD OTHERWISE BE A MERE VULGAR BRAWL!'

DEAR MUM AND DAD

A frequent, but not invariable, pattern of wars in which Britain has taken part is:

(a) An early thoroughgoing defeat, or series of defeats.
(b) Reorganization, reinforcement, resupply, and retraining.
(c) Successful operations.
(d) Peace.

In what the British call the South African War and the South Africans call the Anglo–Boer War, (a), (b) and (c) progressed as was customary; (d) faced the political and military planners with an idiosyncratic problem because the Boers, after being forced to raise three major sieges, were defeated in some set-piece battles, lost their capital Pretoria, and simply continued to fight.

This spirited resistance was equestrian and rural. Hardy, self-reliant farmers, using wide tracts of land that they had known from childhood, operated on the veldt. They harassed and ambushed British communications, played merry hell with isolated garrisons, and tied down troops in numbers many times larger than their own.

One of the countermoves decided upon was the expansion of the British mounted force. There were the regular cavalry, the yeomanry, the Australian, New Zealand, Canadian and English-speaking South African volunteer units of light horse, and there was mounted infantry.

Supplementary measures included the provision of a system of defensible blockhouses. It was to one of these blockhouses, manned by a detachment of the Royal Munster

11

Fusiliers, that a weary subaltern led his mounted infantry one evening. His soldiers thought little of their new role, taking the not unreasonable view that if they had wanted to ride horses they would have joined the bloody cavalry in the first place. Their leader had managed to get them all comprehensively lost. They were thirsty, hungry and tired. The horses were in particularly bad shape and had been without food for two days.

One of the functions of blockhouses was to hold emergency stocks of supplies for itinerant mounted infantry patrols.

The subaltern's first thought was for his hungry horses. He wasted neither time nor words.

'Where's your fodder?' he snapped to the nearest sentry.

'In Tralee wit me mudder,' said the sentry.

SILVER LINING

I F Parson White had an attachment to any recognized
religion, nobody knew of it. He was called Parson within
the battalion because in a modest way he performed
voluntarily the non-theological pastoral functions normally
associated with the better type of country clergyman.

In pre-First World War India this humanitarianism was a
great, but not altogether unqualified, boon. Private White
had an education and would patiently write letters for less
literate comrades, improving upon their dictated sentiments
as he did so. He neither drank nor smoked and used the money
thereby saved to buy little presents, bunches of fruit and such,
for the sick and imprisoned whom he visited assiduously.
When the stupefying boredom of life in the ranks in an Indian
cantonment drove someone to near-suicidal depression,
White would appear quietly with words of reassurance and
encouragement. He put barrack-room drunks to bed, organized children's games among the married families, carried the
rifles of exhausted companions on route marches, and com-
forted the afflicted.

There were those who identified a flaw in all this unrelent-
ing philanthropy. As they saw it, the trouble with Parson
White was that he was too damned cheerful by half. It was
usually good to have him present in times of stress, but he was
apt to have an inhibiting effect on traditionally proved outlets
for the easing of discontent and exasperation. If, for example,
two old friends developed a sudden vicious hatred for each
other in the hot weather and started to settle their differences
physically, it might, arguably, be more beneficial if they beat

13

each other to a pulp and got the venom out of their systems rather than be cajoled into a sullen shaking of hands by the pacifying intervention of an eternally smiling White.

Grousing was another case in point. Some soldiers, good ones too, seemed unable to get through a day without the delivery of a stream of embittered rhetoric about the food, accommodation, climate, officers, NCOs and all other contemporarily relevant aspects of their routine lives. Why not, said some. It might be monotonous but if people chose to let off steam in this fashion, why try to stop them? They did little harm and the mental exertion seemed to cheer them up. It was all very well for the Parson to move in amongst them, beaming with goodwill and optimism and grinding out his repetitive slogan that It Might Have Been Worse, but the well-meant solace he brought them usually led to even more elaborate invective when he was out of earshot.

Holders of these reservations did not express them to White himself. He was too much respected, too well liked, too useful for even the most uncouth among a pretty rough crowd to tell him to his face to pipe down and stop behaving like a bloody fairy godmother. Not, that is, until collective patience snapped after a tragedy in the sergeants' married quarters.

This event was an unoriginal manifestation of a recurrent human dilemma. Sergeant Jackman, an easy-going, intelligent senior NCO, was passionately in love with his wife Hilda. Hilda was a girl in her early twenties who had married Jackman at Aldershot a week before the battalion's departure for India. Jackman had been besotted. She had thought him attractive enough but her acceptance of his approaches had held an element of calculation. The union freed her from a household of oppressive nonconformist bigotry and an indeterminate stint as an underpaid counter assistant in her father's confectionery shop.

Jackman wanted a child. So did she. Their best efforts were unproductive.

She became restless and morose. Jackman tried to enliven her with carefully planned bits of conversation. She was unresponsive. He brought friends to the house. She sulked. He

14

took her to beery nights in the sergeants' mess where there was vigorous dancing of the Lancers, Sir Roger de Coverley and eightsome reels by subservient women with tough partners with waxed moustaches. These occasions were not to Hilda's liking.

Jackman, the signals sergeant, was sent on a course. He was a specialist with the heliograph and flag-signalled semaphore and Morse, but needed revisionary tuition on landline telegraphy. He was an absorbent learner. He returned home two days early because the course was cut short by an outbreak of cholera in Meerut, where he was being trained.

He arrived by gharri at his house. He tiptoed in to surprise Hilda. He did. She was in bed with a corporal in B Company whose name he did not know. Jackman tiptoed out again. He went to the arms *kote* and drew a rifle and fifty rounds of ball ammunition. The guard did not dispute the authority of a sergeant. Jackman shot first his wife, then the unidentified corporal, then himself.

The deaths caused extensive sorrow. Jackman, competent and fair-minded, had been popular. Hilda's good looks and kindliness had been admired. The corporal had been liked. There was much regretful, at times maudlin, talk.

Parson White played his hand badly. His zeal in spreading happiness was felt universally to be misdirected. For the first time in anyone's memory he was told so. It was pointed out to him that this was a proper occasion for grief. Smiling exhortations to be of good cheer were unhelpful.

His barrack room rounded on him as one man when he said ritually that It Might Have Been Worse. How the hell, they wanted to know, could it have been worse?

Parson White beamed at them charitably, and explained. 'If Jackman had come home a day earlier,' he said, 'it would have been *me*.'

THE HEART OF THE MATTER

BRITISH casualties in the early days of the South African War were heavy; mounted Boer commandos with a high standard of marksmanship took on and beat soldiers trained to move ponderously in close formation. They reached a peak after a series of disasters known to the newspapers of the day as Black Week.

Most of the wounded were tended in hospitals in the Cape and in Natal. A collection of the more serious cases was returned by hospital ship to Britain for specialist treatment. One of these patients was a corporal in the Royal Irish Rifles, badly damaged at Stormberg by a Mauser bullet that penetrated the left side of his chest.

Because it was where one of the specialists in chest injuries worked, the corporal was taken to a hospital on the Isle of Wight. Everyone there was as kind to him as could be, but he was lonely. He was far from his home and his regiment, and he had no visitors; a deficiency that was put right by Queen Victoria.

He had assumed that something unusual was about to happen when he noticed one morning that the already unnaturally shining and sterile fixtures in his ward were being buffed up to an even higher standard of splendour. The reason became clear when a small, grave old lady, dressed in black and walking with the help of a stick, was escorted through the door, followed by an extensive entourage.

The Queen was greatly moved when she saw the rows of injured soldiers in their white-painted cots. She was not much given to casual chatter (*vide* her reputation for not being

16

amused in the plural) but on this occasion she felt it appropriate to exchange a few words with one patient, chosen at
random. She picked the corporal.

She couldn't have selected a better man. The corporal, one
of nature's gentlemen, was upset by the old lady's obvious

HOPE DEFERRED

Commander-in-Chief SA, Lord K-tch-n-r (reading latest news from England):
'House up! Grouse plentiful! Yacht racing in full swing! I wonder
when *we* shall get *our* holiday?'

distress. He did his best to put her at her ease. A confused and, on her part, stilted conversation ensued during which it became clear that her general concern for so much suffering was becoming focused upon a central item in his account of what had happened to him. What seemed to trouble her was that if the Boer Mauser bullet had entered his chest an inch farther to the left he would have been a dead man.

He reassured her with gallantry. 'There was no real danger at all,' he explained. 'My heart was in my mouth at the time.'

THE PLEASURE OF THE COMPANY

IT was the opinion of Lieutenant Henry Anstruther that the outbreak of war on the 4 August 1914 had brought about a deterioration in the quality of military life. The Anstruther thesis was based on a comparison of before with after. Before the war he had done about one hour's work a day, could take two months leave a year, hunted and shot in season, and was a warmly received guest in well-staffed houses owned by his social equals. Everyone, or at any rate everyone he wanted anything to do with, knew exactly how to behave in any given set of social or military circumstances.

Trends since 1914 demonstrated that this situation no longer existed. All sorts of oddities were being commissioned. People of higher rank, but from inferior arms of the service, kept ordering him to do things at strange hours of the day and night, insisting with a brutal lack of tact that he bloody well did them. Had he been among his own kind with his regiment in France, he would, of course, have accepted that a general European war might perhaps make some extra demands on the time of a subaltern. But he was not with his regiment in France.

To the withering of the sinews of society had been added a personal indignity. Anstruther was the only officer in the British Army, and probably in any army, to have been kicked in the groin by a mule on 3 August 1914. This experience had for the time being limited his military usefulness. After a long stretch in hospital, ducking questions about his symptoms from well-intentioned female visitors and trying not to lose his temper with male ones jovially offering him a place as a soprano in the Vatican choir, he had been turned into a sort of convalescent, mobile odd-job man, sent at short notice to places he didn't want to go to, to do things he didn't want to do.

He was now sitting on a canvas camp chair outside a tent pitched on a shingle beach behind the butts of a rifle range, in hideous isolation from agreeable human contact.

He had been at the range for ten days. Eleven more were yet to come. When given this task he had assumed that he would live in the mess in the barracks in the nearest town, however inadequate the furnishings and however uncouth the inhabitants. The sapper major in charge of training, ginger moustached and with pink eyeballs, had stamped brusquely on this attempt to head for semi-civilization.

'Listen, laddie,' he had said, 'we have on our hands four battalions of Kitchener's mob* who need to fire their musketry courses in three weeks. The only way to get through it is to use every hour of daylight. The only way to use all the daylight is to have you and the butt party living on the range, ready at dawn and standing down at dusk. Clear?'

It had been clear. Anstruther's batman had drawn a tent from the quartermaster and had set it up on the shingle beach, with a canvas camp bed and a canvas washbasin on a collapsible stand. Hampers ordered from Fortnum and Mason had arrived just in time. There was a supply of suitable wine. Anstruther did not travel to untested places without bringing a stock of his own.

There had been interminable activity since the establishment of this one-officer mess. Each day, from the sun's first rosy rising in the east until its welcome disappearance in the west, had been a boring melange of repetitive routine: the crack and thump of thousands of rifle bullets, clamorous suggestions from the Kitchener's Army colonels for an

---

* 'Kitchener's Army' was raised from volunteers who responded to an appeal ('Your Country Needs You') from Lord Kitchener of Khartoum, appointed as Secretary of State for War in 1914. They are best celebrated in Ian Hay's *The First Hundred Thousand*.

improvement in the services provided, and ill-mannered interventions by the sapper major.

Anstruther went to bed in preparation for a 5 a.m. start. Low waves broke irritatingly with a slapping noise against the shingle and receded with an equally irritating rumble as they shifted the shingle about. Anstruther, weary, fell asleep, undisturbed. He stirred once only, just before dawn, when his subconscious registered a formless crash. He did not awake.

Well before first light his batman brought him a cup of tea and recommended an extra stay in bed. The beach and the range were obliterated by a thick sea mist. The batman would report when it showed signs of clearing. Anstruther gratefully had an additional doze.

At nine o'clock he groped his way to the butts. The butt party, looking pleased with themselves, were playing cards and smoking. He blundered to the farthermost firing point. It was deserted. Kitchener's Army was doubtless also enjoying what in their crude jargon they probably called a late kip. Anstruther made his way with difficulty back to his tent on the beach.

At 10.30 the mist began to clear. By 11.30 the sun had burned it all away. At some point between these two times Anstruther's batman pointed out to sea, said 'Strewth', and added 'sir' later.

Three hundred yards from the tent was a large, unmoving, newly arrived shape. The mist still drifted about patchily, but from glimpses of gun turrets, funnels, masts and other seafaring paraphernalia, Anstruther identified a major unit of the Royal Navy. He thought, rightly, that it was a battle cruiser. He also thought, and also rightly, that it was aground.

He was pleased to see the battle cruiser. It brought a new dimension to his life. His earlier dealings with naval officers had been few, but he had much enjoyed the company of the ones he had met. Unlike the sapper major and most of the Kitchener people, they had been the sort of fellows who wouldn't have looked out of place in his club. They knew how to behave.

The more Anstruther thought about it, the more evident it

21

became that in this possibly unique situation, with him in his tent and them in their battle cruiser, the two separated by only a few hundred yards of water and shingle, he had an obligation to them; to the wardroom, to the captain, and maybe to an admiral as well if there was one, which, judging from the size of the thing, seemed likely.

There was indeed an admiral. At the same time as Anstruther was thinking about the surprise arrival of these welcome intruders to his lonely territory, the admiral was looking at the same phenomenon from a different angle. He had already put almost everyone in sight under open arrest. He had advised suicide as the best next move for the navigator and the officer of the watch. He had shown a heavily ironic interest in how the captain intended to spend the leisure that would soon be his in civilian life, and he was now drafting a reply to a wireless signal from the First Lord of the Admiralty, Mr Winston Churchill.

Mr Churchill's message, which carried a reflective introduction about the execution of Admiral Byng by firing squad in the eighteenth century, was mostly about assurances that he had been given that the battle cruiser was steaming towards the sound of the guns in the Dardanelles. Mr Churchill had now been told that this was not altogether true. For how long did the admiral propose to settle down in his present location? Not to put too fine a point upon it, he, Mr Churchill, could think of more productive uses to which the ship could be put.

The admiral had always been more adept with the sword than with the pen. He resented personal, prodding messages from a civilian Minister. He was searching for a form of words which would put that shifty little opportunist Churchill in his place without imperilling his own now shaky promotion prospects. His arteries became seriously overworked during this literary struggle.

In disciplined hierarchies, emotional extremism spreads downwards, fast. While tugs, tenders and pinnaces gathered to help refloat the ship, and the captain was working out what he would say at the court martial that was mandatory for commanding officers in his situation, the other officers grimly paced about. They infused every order they gave with a vicious malevolence that worked its way with interest through the warrant and petty officers to every corner of the lower deck. It was not a happy morning on the battle cruiser.

To this uncharitable desert of moral desolation rowed Anstruther's batman, in a dinghy. He threaded his way through the assembling craft, climbed the gangway, and asked for advice from the Royal Marine Light Infantry sentry. Who was the senior naval officer aboard? The batman had a letter for him.

The sentry said that that would be the admiral. He worked from somewhere near the stern. The best thing the batman could do was to head that way and keep asking. On more normal days the sergeant of marines would have provided a guide, but the marine detachment were all busy at the moment escorting to the cells seamen who had been charged with prejudicing good order and naval discipline by looking too cheerful while working.

The batman, clutching his letter, went slowly aft. Advice on the last leg of his journey brought him to a marine messenger. The marine looked at him cynically and accepted the letter, prior to delivering it to the admiral's flag lieutenant.

The acceptance coincided with the admiral's bursting blasphemously through an adjacent watertight door in search of fresh air and further subjects for disciplinary reprisal. He saw the batman in his khaki uniform waving a letter about. The admiral snatched the letter threateningly and checked it to see whom it was for. He had a mind to have the addressee imprisoned for wasting time on irrelevancies. He saw that it was for the senior naval officer aboard – himself. He at once began to wonder whether he had gone too far in his telegraphed riposte to Mr Churchill.

If the logic that led to this apprehension lacked body, there were elements in it that, when cobbled together in haste, made superficial sense. The admiral *had* been curter in his signal than he had intended. If My Lords of the Admiralty decided to sack an admiral they would be more likely to do so by means of a sealed letter dispatched by hand than by broad-casting the whole imbroglio over the open airwaves. The messenger was wearing khaki, was clearly not of the ship's company, and was presumably some sort of Royal Marine dispatch rider, sent at speed from Whitehall. He must have moved remarkably fast, but . . . .

The admiral tore open the envelope.

'Mr Henry Anstruther,' he read, 'presents his compliments to the Senior Naval Officer, the Commanding Officer, and the officers of that one of His Majesty's Ships to which this message is being delivered.

'Mr Anstruther apologizes for his inability to designate the vessel with more precision but because of the manner in which the ship is wedged on the sea bottom he has been unable to read the name, which he understands is customarily written by the Royal Navy on the back part.

'Since the back part is at present pointing out to sea at right angles to the shore it is obscured from Mr Anstruther's view.

'During their stay, which Mr Anstruther hopes will be as long as possible, Mr Anstruther cordially invites the ship's officers to become honorary members of his mess.

'The mess is situated on the beach in the tent that, the distance being so short, must be clearly visible from the front of the ship.

'Mr Anstruther takes this opportunity to renew his com-pliments to the Senior Naval Officer, the Commanding Officer and the members of the wardroom.'

The risk that the battle cruiser and its ancillary shifters might be peppered by overs from Kitchener's Army closed the range for the rest of the day. In mid-afternoon the sapper major came to see Anstruther in the tent. Anstruther apologized for his batman's not being present to serve tea. The batman seemed to have been detained on the ship.

'Detained is right,' said the major. 'He's in the lock-up. Medieval crowd, the Navy. They take it out on bearers of bad news. Mind you, they're also pretty thorough about hunting down the originators. They sent a lieutenant ashore in a frock coat with a sword to pick you up too.' He chuckled.

Anstruther stared in puzzlement and said nothing.

'I sent him away with a flea in his ear,' went on the major. 'Told him he had no jurisdiction. The sailors are now putting the whole thing in writing to the Provost Marshal.' The major chuckled again.

Anstruther stayed baffled.

'I hand it to you,' said the major admiringly, 'I'd never have thought up a dodge like that to get out of a dump like this. I was so impressed, I've spent the last couple of hours pulling strings for you. You're off to France tonight, whatever the doctors say. All fixed. I hope to join you soon.'

He wished Anstruther luck and left, still grinning appreciatively.

Anstruther had been unable to understand almost anything of what the major had been talking about. He had, however, absorbed the news that he was at last to be reunited with like-minded brother officers familiar with the nuances of correct social usage. He was immensely cheered. He had one small feeling of regret. He would never develop his planned friendships with the naval officers. They would have been admirably sophisticated companions.

GOLDEN WORDS

Prince Hal, addressing the troops at Harfleur as 'Dear friends', invited them colourfully to accompany him once more into the breach, adding weight to the importance he placed upon the invitation by heady references to Saint George and England.

General Sir Bernard Montgomery, wearing two cap badges, made a habit of telling his followers in the 8th Army to break ranks, gather round, and listen to how he intended setting about hitting Rommel for six.

Between these two peaks there was a bad slump in British military oratory. The record for economy of words is probably held by Field Marshal Lord Kitchener who, as Secretary of State for War in 1915, managed a controlled expenditure of seven while inspecting an infantry brigade of the new army.

The Kitchener oral contribution to this event was: 'Do the steel helmets fit the men?'

THE HALT AND THE LAME

EVEN those many who felt affection for him, and they grew in number after the night he shot the orderly officer outside a supply dump near Basra in 1915, would not claim that Private Wood was an intellectual Titan. Honest and willing, yes. But not very bright.

His nickname of Solid epitomized his comrades' opinions. The doctor, a student of international military affairs, put it more subtly when he said that he doubted whether Wood would have qualified as a recruit to the United States army of the day. Asked what that was supposed to mean, the doctor pointed out that a current statutory minimum requirement for enlistment in the United States Army was a mental age of at least eight.

The court of inquiry convened to look into the shooting of Lieutenant Parker, the orderly officer, assembled with the best of intentions. It was to some extent influenced by two extrajudicial considerations. The first was that the weather was unspeakably, stickily, hot and there was an urge to complete proceedings as soon as possible. The second, although the members of the court were scrupulous in trying to banish it from their minds, was prejudice. Solid Wood's contribution to the safety of the supply dump was seen as an inspired piece of philanthropy, a public-spirited deed long overdue. Anyone who did in Parker, was the feeling, was all right. Given half a chance of getting away with it, all those entrusted with establishing the facts would have done it themselves.

The background facts were not in dispute. Shipping from India made a haphazard delivery to the port of Basra in the

27

Persian Gulf of ammunition, equipment, clothing, food and miscellaneous supplies. The bulk of these was intended for use by the 6th (Poona) Division, commanded by General Townshend. The 6th Division was now fighting Turks several hundred miles farther up the River Tigris than anyone had thought it would, and than anyone sensible had thought it should. The only way to get the stores to Townshend was by river steamer. There were too few. The unsent surplus piled up in Basra, stacked in dumps.

The Mesopotamian Arabs saw this arrangement as a happy bonanza. They plundered the dumps. They were skilled at it.

Sentries on the dumps had accordingly been strengthened. Their orders, read to them before they went on duty by NCOs, were explicit. If strangers approached, a sentry was to 'Call out, "Halt or I fire", three times. If the stranger fails to halt, open fire.'

Solid Wood had opened fire and had shot Parker. The question to be resolved by the court was whether the circumstances were such that Wood was justified in doing so. Alternatively, had his intent been murderous or malicious, or had he been plain careless?

The court's findings would thus be determined by the answers to two subsidiary questions. Could Parker, who was Wood's platoon commander as well as the orderly officer, have reasonably been mistaken for a stranger on a moonlit night by Wood? If so, had Wood used the prescribed formula before shooting?

The answer to the first question, surprisingly, was yes. The identification of Parker could well have been difficult because Parker before leaving on his rounds had confided to a brother officer that he meant to 'catch those idle bloody sentries out'. The Parker belief was that they kept dropping off to sleep. Instead of clattering about openly, Parker would sneak up on them in the dark and would, with luck, confiscate a rifle or two before the slumbering sentries knew what was happening. Consequent sentences of prolonged imprisonment, perhaps even death, should improve the performance of their successors immeasurably.

The court registered this evidence impassively. Privately, the members contemplated the mixture of arrogance, malevolence and dim-wittedness that had characterized the late Parker.

Solid Wood, cross-examined on the nature of Parker's approach in the moonlight, did not help his case much by the cheerful confusion of his replies. Neither did he harm it. The court, realists all, did not expect from him a high level of coherence.

In the matter of whether he had made the challenge correctly, Wood was more impressive. Word for word, he said, no mistake. Confirmation of this came from Corporal Mingay who had heard Wood clearly. No doubt about it, said Mingay, word for word was right.

After a short adjournment the court found that Parker's death was an accident and that no blame attached to Wood. Instructions for the guidance of orderly officers should be revised to prevent a recurrence of the contributory causes of the accident. The court dissolved itself, its members going sweatily to an overdue drink.

Wood, widely congratulated by his mates, seemed modestly puzzled. He'd only done his job, hadn't he? It wasn't often that the job made you learn off a lot of words *and* shoot someone like Parker, but he'd done it and he'd do it again. No more to be said.

Corporal Mingay, whose testimony on Wood's right use of the challenge formula had clinched the issue, kept his own counsel. Mingay had told the exact truth. He had forborne to add that what that silly bugger Wood had done was to call into the night an unpunctuated, meaningless, and painfully memorized set of words that added up to gibberish. 'Halt-or-I-fire-three-times-if-the-stranger-fails-to-halt-open-fire,' Wood had chanted proudly, before dispatching Parker on the last syllable.

Mingay had no complaints about this compressed sequence.

DEUXIÈME SERVICE

DURING the years preceding 1914 large numbers of young German men came to Britain to work in the catering trade. They broadened their experience, earned a little money, and learned to speak English. They were tidy, clean, disciplined and biddable. They were excellent employees. A few were unlucky enough to be interned at the outbreak of war. Most got out in time, returned home, and were mobilized in the German Army.

In 1915 a British brigade commander in France, examining returns submitted to him by his brigade major, was intrigued by some figures put in by one of his four battalions. Successes achieved by this unit's snipers numbered more than those of the other three battalions added together, although the snipers of all four were roughly equal in skill, training and patience.

'We're trying a new system,' explained the colonel of the sniping champions the following day. 'At its closest point we're only fifty yards from the German line. We can hear them talking when the wind's right. The snipers are lying in cover behind our support trench. We've a chap in the fire trench with a very loud voice. When he hears an unusually large number of jerries talking, he shouts "Waiter!" at the top of his voice. There's usually some fellow with conditioned reflexes who looks over the top and calls back "Coming, sir". That's one more on the scoreboard.'

CAVEMAN

THE Allied attempt to shorten the First World War by forcing the Dardanelles foundered largely through mischance and indifferent higher leadership. Another major element in the debacle was the totally underestimated fighting quality of Anatolian peasants conscripted into the Turkish army. They were as difficult to shift from well-dug-in defensive positions as the Japanese were found to be thirty years later.

The Gallipoli operations were gruesome. In some places Turkish trenches were within grenade-throwing range of those of the disembarked British, Australian, New Zealand and Indian troops. Weapons in use ranged from artillery, land and naval, to small arms, bayonets, clubs and boots. Casualties to both sides were enormous.

After several weeks of murderous attrition, with unrecovered dead decomposing in the sun in the narrow space between the opposing lines held raggedly on rocky hillsides, it became clear that the dead themselves were generating a new threat. Unless they were buried soon, destruction by weaponry would be supplemented by a lethal outbreak of disease. Its effects would be indiscriminate. It was in the interests of all participants to do something about it.

The only possible solution to the problem was to call a brief truce during which working parties from each side could clear the battlefield of their dead without interference. It was, of course, important that neither side should exploit the ceasefire to its own tactical advantage. Any arrangements made would require delicate diplomacy, must be

31

TALES FROM THE TRENCHES

*Some of our soldiers, who were within seventy yards of the German
trenches, hoisted an improvised target. The Germans did the same. Both
sides signalled the result of the shooting.*
First Tommy: 'GET DOWN! DO YOU WANT 'EM TO COP YER?'
Second Tommy: 'BLIMEY! THE PERISHERS SIGNALLED MY BULL A
MISS, AND I'M JUST AGOIN' TO 'OP OVER AN' TELL 'EM ABAHT IT'

unambiguous in their description, and must be easy to
implement.

Preliminary feelers put out by the British were favourably
received by the Turks. It was agreed that detailed negotia-
tions should be carried out in a cave behind one of the

Australian positions. The Turkish emissaries, equipped with safe conducts and temporarily blindfolded as they were led through the Australian defences, were taken to the meeting place.

The proceedings were elaborately formal. Representation was from the very top. The Turkish delegation was led by the brilliant young field commander, General Mustapha Kemal Pasha, who was accompanied by his German adviser, General Liman von Sanders. General Sir Archibald Hunter-Weston spoke for the British. All three generals and their supporting staff officers dressed for the occasion as for a ceremonial parade. There was polished leather, and swords, and orders and decorations.

Introductions were made with cold correctness and to an accompaniment of salutes, bows and heel-clicking. It was a glittering little display of military splendour, contrasting sharply with the surrounding squalid realities of twentieth-century land warfare.

Before discussions of substance got under way, twentieth-century warfare, in the shape of an Australian soldier, obtruded. He was very tall, very sunburned, and was casually dressed in a wideawake hat, a pair of boots, and nothing else.

He walked into the cave, looked at the gleaming negotiators without surprise, and addressed them. 'Any of you jokers seen my fucking kettle?'

BULLRING

ALTHOUGH those close to him claimed that he had a subtle mind and a heart of gold, the external furnishings of General Sir Edmund Allenby gave nothing away when it came to suggesting either of these qualities. He was very large, very noisy, and put the fear of God into people with whom he disagreed. He was known as 'the Bull' but not addressed as such, even by his intimates. In 1914 he commanded the Cavalry Division of the British Expeditionary Force in France.

Finding, as he saw it, cause to reproach one of his brigadier generals during the retreat from Mons, General Allenby took this luckless officer aside to tell him in private what he thought of his performance.

His monologue enchanted everyone in hearing of the Bull's idea of a low-toned rebuke, i.e. most of the Cavalry Division, a selection from other formations which had gone astray in the retreat, and miscellaneous passers-by. 'There are fools,' bawled Allenby confidentially, 'there are damned fools, and there is *you*.'

LOVABLE JOCKS

WHETHER or not it was right for Highland regiments to continue to wear the kilt in the glutinous muck of trench warfare in places like Passchendaele in 1916 was a matter, decided English observers, that could be settled only by Scotsmen. The sight of Scottish soldiers plastered up to their bare thighs in a thick casing of mud none the less suggested to Sassenach minds that an early change to trousers would do no harm.

The French Commander in Chief, Marshal Foch, felt nothing parallel to English inhibitions about commenting on this delicate national issue. He summed up the kilt as, *'Bon pour l'amour mais pas pour la guerre.'*

THE SOFT WORD

IT fell to the lot of General William Robertson to pass the news to General Sir Horace Smith-Dorrien that he, Smith-Dorrien, was sacked. Robertson's instructions were to leave no doubt in Smith-Dorrien's mind that his career was over, but to coat the pill with all available sugar. Sympathetic tact was the watchword. Smith-Dorrien's offence had been the embarrassing one of disobeying a direct order, fighting a successful action at Le Cateau in 1914, and saving the British Expeditionary Force. Nelson got away with indiscipline and victory at Copenhagen. Smith-Dorrien did not in Belgium rather more than a hundred years later.

Robertson was an unusual soldier. In an era when the rigidities of class seemed immutable, and nowhere more so than in the army, he had enlisted as a trooper in a cavalry regiment, worked his way rapidly through every rank to sergeant major, and had been commissioned. With neither private financial means nor influential friends in high places, he had then progressed through every commissioned rank and was ultimately to become the wartime Chief of the Imperial General Staff and a field marshal.

He discharged his delicate mission to Smith-Dorrien with the compact efficiency that marked all his enterprises. He did it in the accent that made no concessions to that of the military caste in which he was now prominent.

' 'Orace,' said Robertson, 'you're for the 'igh jump.'

PUFFED WITH PRIDE

THE 2nd Battalion of the Irish Guards was raised in 1915 and based at Warley in Essex. Training was concentrated, thorough and exhausting. Instructions in the basic military skills was complemented by an insistence upon scrupulous personal smartness at all times.

Among the items of equipment subjected to regular critical scrutiny were the big pack and the small pack. (These uncomfortable carrier bags were still in use in the Second World War until some units at least were issued with Bergen frames and rucksacks.) The big pack was worn on the back, held by shoulder straps. The small pack, fastened to the waistbelt, hung to one side. Both were carried simultaneously, along with ammunition pouches, entrenching tools, water bottles and similar impedimenta, when the troops paraded in full marching order. The overall load was heavy.

The packs, which accommodated everything to keep a man warm, nourished and clean when living rough, were required to be faultlessly blancoed. The brass fittings were polished to a high sheen. Packs had to be moulded into the right shape: all surfaces flat and all corners square. Since they were made of webbing, not a stiff material, this took much care and precision in packing.

The battalion fell in in full marching order for a fifteen-mile route march on an exceptionally hot summer's day. Each man was inspected in the closest detail under the brooding supervision of the adjutant. The names of backsliders were recorded by NCOs for subsequent disciplinary sanctions.

All was finally judged to be suitable for departure. A

muffled bang and a hissing noise came from the big pack of an ensign standing motionless in front of his platoon. The pack began slowly to collapse inwards upon itself. It deteriorated into a distressing crumbled thing, lacking straight sides and right-angled corners.

The adjutant went bleakly to investigate this unusual event. The ensign explained that his aversion to carrying heavy weights over long distances was such that he had designed an inflatable rubber filling, shaped to the measurements of his pack. When he had pumped it up that morning he had misjudged the optimum pressure. He had not allowed for expansion brought about by a quite remarkably warm day.

PUT IT DOWN TO EXPENSES

THE battle of Loos, which began on 25 September 1915, was described by propagandists and commentators as the prelude to a major British breakthrough against the Germans in the West. It would, according to this analysis, lead to an early end of the First World War. The analysts were widely believed, and were wrong.

One of the believers was Brigadier General Lord Tullibardine, who commanded the Scottish Horse Brigade at Gallipoli. When he heard the good news, he instructed his brigade, who were dismounted and fighting in trenches as infantry, to give three cheers. They did so.

The Turks in the trenches opposite the Scottish Horse Brigade listened to the cheering and assumed it to be a tribal warming-up before an attack in strength. The Turks mustered every available man to their parapets and opened fire upon the Scottish position.

The Scots in their turn took this aggressiveness to mean that the Turks were about to mount an assault. The Scots manned their line in full and returned the Turkish fire.

Neighbouring units, British and Turkish, reached the wrong conclusions from the evidence before them and began to fire at one another as well. Both sides called for artillery support. The gunners joined in with vigour.

It slowly became apparent to everyone involved that nobody anywhere was doing anything in the least likely to disturb the current equilibrium. The shooting diminished to its normal volume.

Quartermaster-Sergeant: 'THEM AS 'AS BOOTS AS DON'T FIT 'EM AN' DON'T WANT 'EM, 'AND 'EM OVER TO THEM AS 'ASN'T 'OO DOES'

The administrative staff calculated that Lord Tullibardine's spasm of patriotic enthusiasm had cost the British taxpayer £300,000.

FEATHERS AND MINCEMEAT

BEFORE conscription was introduced during the First World War, one of the less savoury facets of British feminine patriotism was expressed in a domestic psychological campaign, designed to shame healthy men of military age into volunteering for the armed forces.

Comely ladies accosted strangers dressed in civilian clothes and presented them contemptuously with white feathers. The distribution of these badges of cowardice was indiscriminate and frequently led to anomalies, as in the case of a man named Crozier.

Crozier, confronted noisily in Piccadilly by a woman who offered him the alternatives of accepting a white feather or of accompanying her to the nearest recruiting centre, meekly chose the latter. On arrival he gave his profession to the recruiting sergeant as 'Major, Regular Army', added that he was currently on seven days' leave from an infantry battalion in Flanders, and returned to Piccadilly, leaving behind him a spectacular row about interfering, time-wasting harridans.

A variant of the white-feather technique, popular among bellicose ladies of the more affluent classes, was the insertion of an advertisement in the personal column of *The Times*, threatening social or sexual sanctions against craven fiancés, lovers and acquaintances.

One such complicated the Anglo-German propaganda contest. 'G.C.T.,' read the message, 'unless you join up *at once* I shall cut you dead. R.H.'

A German newspaper, which acquired copies of *The Times* regularly through neutral Holland, based a withering leading

41

article about the bloodthirsty savagery of English woman-
hood on R.H.'s sentiments. It was the more stirring because of
their translator's rendering of 'cut you dead' as 'hack you to
death'.

TIME BEING OF THE ESSENCE

A T an important phase of the Battle of Loos in 1915,
Timer Simpson's watch stopped. Several consequences flowed from this failure.
Simpson's company of Sikhs, who should have advanced
from their trenches in precise coordination with an artillery
shoot on a German position, were seven minutes late in starting. Because, through an arithmetical miscalculation by a
gunner officer, one complete field battery was firing short, the
delay saved a massacre of Sikhs by their own support. A
fortuitous coinciding of the gunners' correcting their error at
the same moment that Simpson noticed that something was
wrong with his watch turned a potential fiasco into an entirely
successful attack.

Simpson was congratulated warmly for his acumen in
delaying his start until he had satisfied himself that the guns
were ranging accurately. He was decorated for the vigour with
which he had pressed home his assault.

He could see little point in disclosing that in the noise and
confusion he had misidentified the shortfalling shells as German ones coming the other way, that if his watch had
matched its advertised claims he would have led his company
to destruction on time, or that on the whole he'd had a rather
lucky morning.

The incident left a deep impression on his mind. He had got
away once with a faulty watch but that sort of good fortune
was unlikely to repeat itself. He became obsessive about
always knowing the exact time to the nearest second. From
that day on he wore two watches, one on each wrist. He

compared their readings several times an hour and checked them both against any other timepiece that came in sight. A discrepancy of a second or two would anger him immoderately. His nickname of Timer dated from that period.

Simpson carried his obsession with him throughout the rest of the war and back to peacetime soldiering in India. He accepted good-heartedly a certain amount of heavy humour directed at his foible. After initial disorientation, he became adept at recognizing for what they were the efforts of practical jokers who got up in the middle of the night to confuse him by moving the hands of the four massive clocks, parting gifts from bygone departing commanding officers, that chimed in noisy unison in the officers' mess.

As the years passed, the jokes faded away. Boredom with their repetition aside, Timer Simpson was becoming too old and too senior to have his leg pulled with impunity. He had developed into a comfortable, conscientious, on occasion fierce, middle-aged officer, slowly working his way up the regimental promotion ladder, possessed of a single ambition. He wanted to end his career in command of his battalion. He had evaded deftly attempts to sidetrack him into various staff jobs. He held no illusions about his own limitations. The dizzy heights of the red-hatted command of a brigade or of a division were not for the likes of him.

But to his own Sikhs, men with whom he had grown up, and led into action in France and Mesopotamia, and cherished in training, and shared jokes and countless marches with, and played hockey and shot game with, men whose fathers and grandfathers had served in the regiment, he would, he knew, be a good, firm, just, kindly and efficient commanding officer.

When his promotion duly came through, he was all those things. The battalion when he took it over was in excellent condition. On his retirement three years later it was in equally excellent condition. His one distinctive contribution to a highly professional organism that prided itself on its capacity to maintain its standards through corporate inherent virtue and continuity, not much disturbed by the vagaries of transient commanders whose provenance as one of their own

44

guaranteed their respectability, was the enhancement of their reputation for split-second timing.

During the Simpson era, junior officers constantly looked at their watches. The daily bugle calls were blown precisely when they should have been, not five seconds early or two seconds late. When the battalion paraded ceremonially, or marched out for exercises, it did so on the dot. Senior visitors, the brigade or area commander, were furnished with the customary itemized programmes, but any tendency to linger over something interesting was countered by a courteously ruthless insistence that the loiterer, however exalted, was now due to move to the next event prepared for him. Throughout these unfolding events Timer Simpson still wore his two watches.

His approaching retirement was for him a sadness that, like countless others in his situation, he accepted with a dogged realism. He would shortly leave a large, lively, self-sustaining family, whose triumphs, sorrows, adventures, quarrels, prejudices and eccentricities had absorbed him for almost all his adult life. At his going there would be endless little ceremonies of a high emotional content. There would be a period of formidable eating and drinking, and much reminiscent speech-making, and a glittering farewell battalion parade. Then, on his last day, looking impassive and feeling drained, he would be garlanded with flowers and towed in his car out of barracks by King's and Viceroy's commissioned officers heaving on ropes through a throng of Sikh soldiers, some weeping.

After that, what? A recuperative sea voyage followed by prolonged obscurity without responsibility, combing the household accounts in search of avoidable extravagancies and trying not to sound too much like a pompous old buffer.

To one aspect of these coming valedictions Timer Simpson gave hard thought. It was a regimental custom that departing commanding officers should present to the mess some small memento that was at once decorative, useful and, because of the itinerant nature of soldiering, portable. These limitations and, frankly, a lack of imagination by some of his predecessors had led to an increasingly sterile series of duplications. There were too many candlesticks, cigarette boxes, elaborately worked inkwell sets and silver table centrepiece lumps of statuary depicting Sikhs sticking pigs or shooting tigers. There was also the matter of the four large chiming clocks. The donor of the first had shown a thoughtful originality. The next three were a redundant nuisance. Timer Simpson would like to be remembered as Timer, but to present a fifth clock would be ridiculous.

The idea came to him in bed one morning shortly after he awoke. The more he considered it the more apt it seemed. His legacy to the mess would be unusual, durable, and would provide the true time with a consistent accuracy not dependent upon wayward machinery. Its design and assembly would be fun. It also offered a bonus. Its procurement would require the collaboration of Sikh craftsmen, recruited in circumstances of intrigue and secrecy that his Sikh soldiers loved.

After breakfast Timer listed his specifications to the subhadar major, who smiled in conspiratorial pleasure. He suggested that Lance Naik Mahinder Singh's uncle in Amritsar, who had himself served in the regiment for twenty-one years, should do the brasswork. He was a near genius at it. Jemadar Dillon Singh's brother was the best man with stone. He could shape it in three parts, the centre one fitting the other two, the whole capable of being dismantled for ease of movement.

The components were delivered and ready for assembly on the morning of the day before the mess dined out Timer Simpson. There was strange activity on the south lawn, beyond the mess verandah. Six soldiers arrived and put up a bell tent on a spot pointed out to them by the colonel sahib. The subhadar major, accompanied by four senior NCOs and Dillon Singh's brother, drove up in a fifteen-hundredweight truck and unloaded four wooden boxes, two spades and a wheelbarrow. They disappeared inside the tent. Timer pottered about on the lawn taking bearings with a prismatic compass, withdrawing to the tent at intervals to issue quiet instructions. The signals havildar brought a ladder, a reel of wire and a spotlight, which was fastened by two signallers to a

46

high branch of a tree and focused on the tent. Timer's orderly came with cleaning rags and a tin of metal polish. The occasional clink of a hammer hitting stone was heard.

These happenings were ignored by everyone but the participants. Timer's authority was still absolute. He had ordained that he wanted neither interference nor inquiry.

Timer thanked the working party. The tent flap was fastened. They all went away.

The dining-out on the following evening was a magnificently colourful affair of mess jackets and miniature medals and burnished silver and shining crystal and fine-looking, bearded, puggareed, uniformed mess waiters of discreet efficiency. After the loyal toast, cigars and cigarettes were lit. The port circulated. Brief speeches were made.

Timer ended his, a humorous, nostalgic message of thanks for the past and good wishes for the future, by saying that he had a request to make. He would be gratified, he said, if everyone would follow him to the south garden. He would there unveil a little surprise that he had thought up for them.

They clattered after him in noisy good humour, cigars glowing, glasses clutched. The subhadar major ran the performance with style. The spotlight lit up the bell tent. A soldier unlaced the flap, went inside and grasped the central pole. Other soldiers grasped the canvas skirt, briskly pulled up the tent pegs and stood upright. The subhadar major rasped an order. The soldiers stepped off in unison and marched the tent into the darkness.

The spotlight played on Timer's commemorative sundial, to spontaneous applause. Timer explained enthusiastically that it could be taken to pieces and set up again whenever the battalion moved. The ingenuity of this was favourably commented upon. Timer beamed.

They all walked slowly towards the new mess asset. Timer, as the giver, courteously brought up the rear.

The first person to reach it was the second in command, a considerate, quick-thinking man. He admired the intricately fashioned stone base and the artistry of the brasswork. He read the short inscription on a brass plate set gracefully at the top. He read the equally brief inscription on another brass plate fastened more crudely below the first. Then he turned away, strolled smoothly towards Timer, still at the back of the crowd, and took him firmly by the elbow.

'Colonel,' he said, formally, affably and with lying fluency, 'I am now about to commit an act of insubordination. My old grandmother was Scottish. She believed in ghosts and fairies and things. One of her superstitions was that if anyone who gave a sundial to somebody else looked at the thing by artificial light within three days of handing it over it brought the most appalling bad luck. I'll now take you inside and give you a whisky and soda.'

Timer, mildly put out, deeply incredulous about the likelihood of sufficient numbers of Scotsmen giving sundials to one another for a superstition to have grown about the practice, allowed himself to be led placidly away. He was content. He had seen already from the general laughing reaction that the trouble he had taken in devising his gift had been well thought of.

It was the second, amateurishly fastened, brass notice that had worried the second in command. The first had read simply: 'Presented by Lieutenant Colonel B. J. Simpson MC, 12.x.'37.' The other one said: 'This fucking thing is five minutes fast.'

PASSWORD

IN 1920, when Ireland was embroiled in what is now known variously as the Black and Tan War, the Struggle for Independence, the Anglo-Irish War, or as another instance of the disagreeable ambivalence that dispirits the military in aid to the civil power, depending upon who writes the history and what they think of it, a curfew was imposed in Dublin. All unauthorized persons were to be off the streets by 9 p.m.

This measure was enforced by British troops, accoutred rather extravagantly for the task in steel helmets and webbing equipment as used in trench warfare in 1918. The soldiers carried rifles with bayonets fixed.

Through a series of coincidental mischances a returning group of theatregoers were without a watch between them. They were uneasily conscious that curfew time was either due or overdue. They knew that they had lingered too long in applauding repeated encores after the show. They thought that they might just get home before the evil hour, but they were apprehensive. They were right to be so.

As they moved edgily along the street, a large figure in a tin hat sprang from a shop doorway. He pointed his bayonet at them in an unnerving manner and bawled, '*'Alt. 'Oo goes theyah?*'

There was a silence of mixed embarrassment and nervousness. It was broken by a sobbing feminine voice. 'Jesus, Mary and Joseph!' she said distractedly.

The soldier lowered his bayonet but not his voice. '*'Oly Family pass*,' he roared. '*All's well.*'

49

AND THE SAME TO YOU

HER Britannic Majesty's Ambassador in Addis Ababa, in private life a devotee of health and horses, was in the habit of riding one of the latter every morning before he began his day's work. For the past week his exercise had been conducted against a thumping background of distant martial music which, to his satisfaction, was improving in quality as the days went by.

His pleasure was professional as much as it was aesthetic. A modest component in a small Anglo-Ethiopian military aid programme had been the loan of a British Army bandmaster, charged with the improvement of the performance of Abyssinian regimental musicians.

It had been one of the few arrangements in international or any other form of life that had left all parties happy. The cost to the British taxpayer was derisory. Domestic pacifist critics and foreign disaffected busybodies could find no cause for complaint about neo-colonialist merchants of death inciting peace-loving Africans to murder one another. The bandmaster was able to combine a relaxed change of scene with some gratifying, enjoyable work with an audible end product.

The bandmaster was a small, smart man with a straight back. He had, years before, enlisted as a boy musician. He was a no-nonsense perfectionist who took things one at a time. With him there was no flighty darting about from one musical work to another. He had started off his new students on 'Colonel Bogey' and they would stay with it until they had achieved mastery. Then, and no earlier, they would move on to a repetitive attack on 'The Lincolnshire Poacher'.

CO (to delinquent brought up for having a dirty rifle): 'AH! A *VERY* OLD SOLDIER! I SUPPOSE YOU MADE YOURSELF OUT TO BE YEARS YOUNGER THAN YOU ARE WHEN YOU RE-ENLISTED. WELL, WHAT WERE YOU CHARGED WITH THE LAST TIME YOU WERE BROUGHT UP TO THE ORDERLY ROOM?'
Delinquent (stung to irony): '''AVIN' A DIRTY BOW AN' ARRER, SIR!'

'Coloney Bogey' had by now echoed around the plateau in several hundred oompah-ed renderings. It was nearly as good as it ever would be.

A horseman cantered towards the ambassador from the direction of the music. As he approached, the ambassador recognized the Ethiopian liaison officer to the band project, a courteous and ambitious young captain. Aside from doing his liaison job efficiently, the captain had sensibly been making the most of his dealings with the bandmaster to add to his limited English vocabulary. It was another useful by-product of the aid scheme.

The captain reined in and saluted.

'Good morning,' said the ambassador genially. 'They're playing very well today.'

'Bollocks, Excellency,' said the liaison officer proudly.

51

HORSE LOVERS

TWO officers conspicuously lacking in the sentimental distress that was prevalent when the military horse was in its last stages of replacement by mechanized transport in the 1930s were the colonel and the adjutant of a Gurkha battalion stationed in India. They knew their limitations. They and horses were incompatible. There was mutual misunderstanding, incomprehension and ignorance of each other's working parts.

Only two horses were left to each infantry battalion. The commanding officer and his adjutant were required to ride them on prescribed occasions such as ceremonial parades.

One of these parades began unremarkably. The battalion fell in by companies, took up its dressing smartly from the right, was inspected by the company commanders and stood rigid and glittering in the sunshine. The adjutant sat gingerly in his saddle and watched the proceedings, his mount shifting uneasily from time to time. He trotted along the front of the parade to listen to the reports of the company commanders. Assured that all was in order, he set about his next task with conditional confidence. He was to gallop forward from the middle of the parade, execute a dramatic-looking skidding halt in front of the colonel, salute with his sword, and announce in a penetrating soldierly voice that the battalion was present, correct and awaiting inspection.

The colonel straddled his mount impassively, hoping to God that it would remain as immobile as it so far mercifully had. He stared sternly to his front and prepared to return the salute. He was disconcerted to find that either the adjutant or

52

the adjutant's horse had made a last-minute change of plan. Instead of pulling up in a cloud of dust in front of him, they persisted in their enthusiastic gallop, passed to his left, and disappeared somewhere to his rear. The colonel, still gazing straight ahead, was considering the implications of this divergence from traditional practice when he received a fierce blow in the small of the back. He was thrown forward violently onto his horse's withers and found himself pinned there by what appeared to be two horse's hooves. There was much inexplicable rhythmic movement.

The adjutant also was in unusual circumstances. A few seconds previously he had been galloping optimistically towards his commanding officer, concentrating upon the precise spot where he would start to rein in, conscious that the disciplined but sardonic eyes of seven hundred Gurkha soldiers were watching his back view with interest. Now he was high in the air, sword in hand, and contemplating his audience. His horse was copulating vigorously with the colonel's mare. Both men, and both horses, were trapped in a strange vibrating tableau, like an obscene parody of a piece of Victorian heroic equestrian statuary.

The adjutant made some swift mental calculations. If he dismounted he would not free the entrapped colonel, the upper half of whose body had now slid round to the left and who, with both arms clasped around the mare's neck, was looking upwards bitterly. The adjutant decided that since there was nothing practical that he could do to ameliorate the immediate stalemate he might as well make the most of his opportunity to examine the soldiers from an altitude that until now had been denied him. He stayed where he was, heaving in the swell, looking carefully at the faces of the troops in a slow progression from right to left. He was responsible for discipline and he checked for signs of insubordinate amusement. He was proud to see that there was none.

The colonel, a realist, put a pertinent question to the adjutant. What, he wanted to know, was the customary duration of the equine sex act? The adjutant lowered his glance to the upturned face several feet below him and said respectfully

53

that he didn't know, but that this one seemed to have been going on for longer than he had thought possible.

The second in command now intervened. He marched at a steady pace to the scene of the action, saluted the colonel stylishly, and asked for permission to investigate the problem. The colonel urged him to do so. The second in command carried out a detailed examination of the heart of the matter, thought out his next move, and announced his conclusions in a carrying voice.

'Hold on, sir,' he roared, 'I'll try hitting him on the cock with my stick.'

The adjutant, alerted to a new threat to discipline, stared sharply at the parade again. The company commanders were taking no more chances.

'*A Compan-ee*,' bawled the first one, '*ay-bout turn!*'

'*B Compan-ee, ay-bout turn!*'

'*C Compan-ee. . . .*'

The details of the tableau's disentanglement remained a three-man confidence. The discipline of a unit of the old British-Indian Army remained intact.

BREAD OF HEAVEN

AMONG the mail sorted by the orderly room clerk on a chilly December morning in the early 1930s was an envelope addressed to God, c/o the Depot, Royal Welch Fusiliers, Wrexham.

The lance corporal clerk knew a dilemma when he saw one. People in hierarchical organizations can show an abrasive sensitivity if asked, however tactfully, if they are the right recipients of correspondence intended for God. An alternative ploy of simply putting the letter without comment in the in-tray of the adjutant or the regimental sergeant major could invite a charge of dumb insolence. To open it himself could be similarly perilous. Just who the hell, the question might be put, did he think he was?

The clerk solved his problem by inertia. He put the letter to one side of his desk, distributed the rest of the mail, and set about his next task, the making of tea. The orderly room sergeant, passing idly by, saw the letter and picked it up. It found its way, through the correct channels, to the commanding officer.

The commanding officer was an ageing, resolute major, untroubled by reservations. He opened the letter on the grounds that, communication difficulties being what they were, (a) God wouldn't get the message unless someone read it first, (b) he, the major, was the nearest thing in the depot to God, so reading it was clearly his responsibility, (c) the means of transmission could be determined only when the nature of what had to be passed on had been established.

55

The letter was unambiguous. Its signatory was 'Williams 67'. Williams 67 was in trouble.

The major had known Williams 67 for a very long time. Williams 67, called so by the last two digits of his army number to differentiate him from all the other Williamses in a Welsh regiment, had been with the major in France. He was an old friend and an old adversary. The major, as a young platoon commander, had recommended Williams for the Distinguished Conduct Medal for exceptional resourcefulness and gallantry on the Somme and had not been too dissatisfied when Williams was awarded the lesser (but still greatly respected) Military Medal. Later, when he was a company commander in India, the major had dealt severely with repetitive disciplinary offences committed by Williams, most of them of interesting originality and all of them to do with strong liquor, illegal gambling, and out-of-bounds women. The major, not given to the casual expression of praise, had several times commended Williams as the best turned-out man on parade. A long-gone padre had once described Williams, when sober, as the most genuinely religious man he had ever met.

There had been long periods when Williams had eschewed sin and taken to study. He had passed the examinations for all his army educational certificates, following each success by a celebratory outbreak that added to the length of his conduct sheet.

Williams, in short, had been a regimental character – complex, unpredictable, totally reliable when reliability was important, haphazardly irresponsible when it wasn't. The major would never have admitted it to anyone, but he felt a deep, respectful, grateful love for Williams 67 and all his kind.

For the past eight years Williams, after twenty-five years' service, had been living on a tiny pension in a small town in North Wales. The major reread the letter.

Dear God,

As You well know, I have had difficulties in my time and have usually got out of them by my own efforts with Your help. This time it's different. All my efforts have been of no avail. I must rely entirely on You. . . .

There followed an account of Williams's current troubles, which were financial. His pittance of a pension, supplemented by occasional payments for such odd jobs as he was able to get during the Depression, was insufficient to sustain a modest programme of drinking pints and backing losing horses. An erosion of cash had been succeeded by a suspension of credit. Unless he could settle outstanding debts for coal, gas and groceries, he would face an unpleasant and, at his age, possibly a lethal winter.

The means-testing predecessors of the Welfare State could do nothing for him. The British Legion had been sympathetic to the plight of an old soldier and had given him a small subsidy, but rightly, as Williams told God without rancour, were using their limited funds to help ex-servicemen who were disabled or had families to look after. Williams would not seek help from any other human source. Pride was sinful but self-respect was not. He had accordingly decided to put the matter into the hands of God. He attached an appendix that listed the sums owed. The total was £15.

The major was not a rich man. He had two children, Christmas was coming up, and the spring term's school fees were due, payable in advance. But he could not let down Williams 67. Neither could he afford £15.

He spoke elliptically to the adjutant about Christmas, and stupid old soldiers the salt of the earth, and no obligation on anyone, and the need for anonymity to preserve an old man's pride.

The adjutant's consultation with the RSM, and the subsequent involvement of the orderly room sergeant and the lance corporal clerk were similarly unspecific. No suggestions were made. Certainly no orders were given. A large brown envelope circulated. It was left on individual desks when their owners were absent. There were careful, private calculations of what an underpaid warrior of the 1930s could subscribe, how much to add for luck, and of the best time to leave the envelope on somebody else's desk without being seen.

The RSM, another old friend and enemy of Williams, brought the envelope to the major. The major did some legerdemain from his wallet, put five one-pound notes in the envelope while the RSM looked the other way, and said, 'Count it, now.'

'I think that's right, sir,' said the RSM.

There were nine pounds, twelve shillings. The major emptied the small change from his pockets. So did the RSM. They counted again.

'Ten pounds, one shilling,' said the major.

'You take the shilling back, sir,' said the RSM. 'Keep it neat. Round tenner.'

'How do we get it to him? We can't forge a letter from God. He'd get suspicious.'

They thought it over. They agreed the solution was to change the money into ten one-pound notes, and to post them without a covering letter.

An unnatural feeling of seasonal goodwill and self-satisfaction settled over the orderly room.

A further letter addressed to God, c/o the Depot, arrived some days later. Before opening it the major, normally a stickler for the proprieties, called in his fellow-conspirators. He read it aloud to them.

Dear God,

I knew You wouldn't fail me. You never have. The money arrived just in time. Thank You.

There is one thing I should let You know. Only ten pounds of the fifteen I asked for were in the envelope. Those thieving bastards in the orderly room must have pinched the other fiver.

Yours sincerely,
B. Williams 67

WHOSE MOVE?

LEVELLERS of accusations that he had always been as
arrogant, self-centred, and bloody-minded as he was as
a field marshal were prone to quote an allegation about
Montgomery's behaviour when, as a lieutenant colonel, he
commanded a battalion of the Royal Warwickshire Regiment
in India in the 1930s.

Montgomery, who thought deeply about all things military, had reached the conclusion that far too much contemporary emphasis was devoted to the minutiae of parade-
ground drill. Drill, in the Montgomery estimation, had its
uses in that bodies of men could be moved from one place to
another in an orderly manner. To turn it into a fetish, by
which the efficiency of a unit was judged by its dexterity on
parade, was absurd.

A consequence of its commanding officer's convictions was
that the Royal Warwicks were not very good ceremonially.
This distressed the brigade commander, late of the Grenadier
Guards, who was.

The brigadier was moved to express his dissatisfaction
publicly at a parade when he noted that Colonel Montgomery, having reported his battalion as present, correct and
awaiting inspection, was not standing where he should have
been standing, which was in front of the precise centre of the
troops lined up behind him.

The brigadier gave voice to a calculation that Colonel
Montgomery was six paces to the left of where he should
have been. He told the colonel to correct this error, in
the meanwhile deferring the next stage of his inspection

59

MESOPOTAMIA

Tommy (to padre, who has been telling him about the scriptural associations connected with the country): 'SUPPOSED TO BE THE GARDEN OF EDEN, IS IT, SIR? WELL, IT WOULDN'T TAKE NO FLAMIN' SWORD TO KEEP *ME* OUT OF IT'

until Montgomery had moved six paces to his right. Colonel Montgomery stood his ground and ordered the five hundred strong 1st Battalion of the Royal Warwickshire Regiment to move six paces to its left.

THE LOST LEADER

THE largest volunteer fighting force in the history of warfare was formed in India between 1939 and 1945. Its nucleus was the old regular Indian Army. Its expansion required large numbers of junior officers. Some of these were Indian. Others were chosen from promising candidates enlisted in the British Army. These latter were mostly sent to officer cadet training units in India. There, in addition to learning the standard skills of their trade, they could study at first hand the languages, customs and religious inhibitions of the soldiers they would lead in action.

A group of forty of these young men embarked on a troopship at Greenock in 1941. The ship was crowded, uncomfortable and stuffy. The convoy's journey round the Cape seemed interminable. It zigzagged its wearisome, U-boat evading way to almost within sight of North America before turning south and putting in at Cape Town after five weeks' sailing.

There the ships bunkered. The troops, cramped, bored and by now generally bloody-minded, were allowed ashore in batches. The people of Cape Town were hospitable. Official arrangements were tolerant. So long as the shore parties did not become too conspicuously exuberant, and so long as they re-embarked at the times laid down, they were left to their own devices. Parties of military police stood casually about to make sure that the rules of the game were observed.

A body excepted from this civilized loosening of reins was the party of Indian Army cadets. Their conducting officer, Captain Thirsk, had, as he saw it, a more constructive idea.

Captain Thirsk was not a well-loved man. He had come to

his present task not because of a special talent for the education
of potential military leaders but because he was a spare passenger on his way to an administrative headquarters in New
Delhi and had no shipboard responsibilities. The OC Troops,
a tidy-minded re-employed major, had picked Thirsk's name
from a list of officers with nothing to do. The requirements of
the job, as conceived by the OC Troops, were undemanding.
Thirsk would be the agent through whom specific orders and
wishes, outside those embraced by the general routine
ordained for all passengers, would be passed to the cadets. He
could also, provided that he kept it short, be their spokesman
in matters of welfare and morale.

Thirsk saw his function in a more elaborate, missionary
light. Ulcers and astigmatism might have condemned him to
an entirely sedentary form of warfare, but by God he knew his
duty. He would make it his personal business to transmogrify
these scatter-brained young cadets into the smartest, shiniest,
gleamingest draft ever to disembark from a troopship at Bombay. Leaders could only lead effectively if they demonstrably
excelled the led, couldn't they? Sea voyages were notoriously
debilitating, weren't they? Well, Thirsk would soon deal with
that.

Five weeks of polishing, burnishing, ironing and parading,
interspersed with helpful homilies about the need to keep their
bowels in good working order and advice on the way to
develop a sense of responsibility did not enchant the embryo
successors of Clive and Bobs Bahadur. They neither mutinied
nor protested. They did develop a sophisticated plan to push
Thirsk over the side by night but, like many a good plan, it
came to nothing. Thirsk habitually went early to bed to rest
his duodenum.

Thirsk's Cape Town programme was about what the
cadets had expected it to be. To brisk cries from their commander, they fell in on the jetty. They were given a pep talk.
Their soldierly appearance, he said, did both him and them
credit. The privileges of officers carried concomitant responsibilities. They would now demonstrate both simultaneously.
Led by Thirsk, they would march to attention through the

streets of the city, giving a display of parade-ground virtuosity that would enhance their pride in themselves, would inspire and perhaps shame some of those slovenly other ranks now racketing around the local fleshpots, and would impress the South African public. The latter, let's face it, were basically colonials but there was no reason to suppose that some of them at least weren't bad chaps. *'Move* to the *right* in *threes. Ri-i-i-ght turn. Ker-wi-i-ck maarch.'*

The early stages of their progress were much admired. Thirsk, short, smart and immaculately turned out, staring grimly straight ahead, marched five paces in front of his little column, swagger stick tucked under his left armpit, left arm still, right arm swinging shoulder high. Behind him the cadets swung both arms shoulder high. From time to time, as they passed an object or person of suitable respectability, a war memorial or an officer of field rank, Thirsk's resonant barrack-square voice would give the order 'Eyes right'. As his hand came up vibrantly in salute, his head, and the heads of all the cadets other than the right marker, would jerk to the right in beautiful synchronization. They stayed so placed until whipped back again in unison by the 'Eyes front' from Thirsk.

It was after the completion of the fourth of these military greetings that the squad, once more able to look where they were going, began to realize that something was on. Their leader, the iridescent Thirsk, was no longer the regulation five paces ahead of them. The distance was nearer to six and a half paces. The right marker, excused by commonsense custom from turning his eyes to the right with everyone else because if he did so the whole lot might stumble sightlessly into an unforeseen obstacle, was putting into practice an exhortation that had echoed around all their heads in a variety of recruit depots. He was using his ferkininitiative. They responded with a warm and full cooperation.

This sage had been doing some mental arithmetic. On formal occasions, the British Army, with the exception of some eccentric rifle regiments, marches at the rate of 120 paces to the minute. Each pace is 30 inches. The distance covered in one minute is thus $\frac{120 \times 30}{12 \times 3}$ = 100 yards. If the marchers shorten their pace by one inch the calculation becomes $\frac{120 \times 29}{12 \times 3}$ = 96 yards 2 feet, a loss per minute of 3 yards 1 foot. The right marker had shortened the pace.

So long as the truncation of the step length is coordinated, the loss in yardage is imperceptible to the casual onlooker. It only becomes noticeable when the man in front begins slowly to draw ahead. Thirsk, staring martially forward, crashing down his heels at 30-inch intervals, did exactly that.

After five minutes Thirsk, still occasionally roaring 'Eyes right' and saluting, was 16 yards and 2 feet in the lead. After seven minutes a taxi and a truck cut between him and his followers, an intrusion of which he was unaware. After ten minutes his orders from 33 yards and 1 foot were barely audible above the hubbub of a Cape Town working day.

The squad lost him at a crossroads. He was at the heel of a departing line of traffic. They, at the head of a stream of further vehicles, were held up by a policeman on point duty. They had a last glimpse of their leader, marching in arm-swinging isolation along the inner traffic lane of a crowded city street, saluting with verve a passing captain of the Royal Navy. They could faintly hear him bawling 'Cadet squ-a-a-ad, eye-e-es *right*' as he did so.

When the traffic policeman turned to beckon them onwards, the cadets wheeled smartly into a left-hand turn. Bereft of their true commander, they took their drill orders from the right marker, making it clear that this was a device of convenience and not an acceptance of his personal authority. They halted by acclamation at the first bar they reached. Further moves, decided by soviet, were settled upon inside.

At about 6 p.m. the OC Troops felt a lift of the heart. For the past hour he had been watching with experienced resignation the return to the ship of a hoarse horde of dishevelled revellers, smelling of beer and emitting turbulent bursts of song. The more serious cases were being helped by friends and reminded the major poignantly of distant days as a subaltern going up the line in the Ypres salient, passing walking

wounded on their way out. Military policemen were conducting the less amenable survivors with cold-hearted brusquerie.
It was all deplorably familiar.

Into this scene of ill-disciplined squalor marched the
Indian Army officer cadet squad, smart as paint and crash-
ingly in step. They halted with a united thud of boots at the
foot of the gangway. A quiet order came from the right
marker, a tall youth whom the major decided to invite to his
cabin at a later date for a drink. The squad turned right as one
man, paused, broke off, and filed elegantly up the gangway.

The major considered this display of disciplined self-
reliance to be the more creditable because the clown nomi-
nally responsible for these splendid young men, some chap
named Thirsk, had set them the worst possible example.
Thirsk was currently under open arrest in the sickbay. The
major had no patience with officers who began their libations
at breakfast time before going ashore in a Commonwealth
country full of disaffected Dutchmen. The fellow couldn't
have mounted a more embarrassing debacle if he'd planned it
deliberately.

The major hadn't so far had time to look into the affair in all
its horrible detail. What he *had* heard was enough for him.
Thirsk marching about like a music-hall comedian, shouting
orders to imaginary soldiers, saluting everything in sight,
disrupting traffic. All that was inexcusable.

But it was small stuff when compared with Thirsk's attempt
to sign the book at Government House. As the major understood it, Thirsk had swaggered, shouting, to the gate lodge,
beside which the book was housed in a sort of sentry-box
thing. Thirsk had bawled, 'Cadet squad, halt,' just as the
Governor General's car, flag flying, had come down the drive.

Thirsk had then put on an insulting pantomime. He had exe-
cuted a parade-ground turn to the right, roared, 'Squa-a-ad,
right *turn*,' gaped, and with the Governor General's car slow-
ing for the gates and with the Governor General staring at him
at two yards range through the open window, had bellowed,
'Jesus Christ, they're gone.'

The South African guard, turned out for the Governor

General's departure, had been presenting arms at the time. Its sergeant had taken no chances with a lunatic blasphemer. He had called, 'Guard, stand fast,' dropped his rifle, sprinted at Thirsk, and felled him with a crashing rugby tackle.

The ADC's report of the incident recorded that at this point he had ordered the driver to accelerate out of the fracas. Thirsk, pinned to the ground by what looked like a Springbok second-row forward, was noisily putting him on a charge for insubordination.

Thirsk's later return to the ship hadn't done much for decorum either. His uniform was filthy, he had a black eye, and he was struggling fitfully with his escort, two bleak, large South African officers.

Enough of the ghastly Thirsk for the moment, reflected the major. Time to think about something more satisfying. That magnificent bunch of young Indian Army officer cadets. . . .

TWO CHEERS FOR CAMPBELL

THE hereditary chief of the Campbells is the Duke of Argyll. In the late seventeenth century, after the last of the Stuart kings lost his throne to his Protestant son-in-law, William III, the Campbells were among those Highlanders who welcomed the change without hesitation. Others, including the MacDonalds, were less enthusiastic. They were given a date by which they should affirm their loyalty to the new regime. The MacDonalds were tardy in doing so, although it is arguable that the delay was technical rather than of substance. The Campbells were authorized to bring them to heel. There followed the massacre of Glencoe in which large numbers of MacDonalds were slaughtered, some while they slept. An element of peculiar treachery characterized these proceedings. Most of the Campbells who did the killings had for some days previously enjoyed the hospitality of their victims. Massacre was compounded by a breach of an ancient Highland code.

In 1940, two hundred and fifty years after Glencoe, a Combined Operations Training Centre was established at Inveraray, the seat of the Duke of Argyll. For the purposes of this specialized school, the physical amenities were as good as could be found in the British Isles. Landing craft could manoeuvre in the sea loch. Beaches were suitable for running troops ashore. There was an enormous acreage of rough country available for field firing exercises, tactical training, and simply marching about, living off the land, and getting fit and self-reliant.

The Royal Marine Brigade arrived to benefit from these attractions earlier than most. With them were the 8th Battalion of the Argyll and Sutherland Highlanders, recruited locally from men who had grown up in the area, knew the hills and valleys backwards, and knew a thing or two about making themselves comfortable in unpromising circumstances. The marines learned much from these hardy characters.

Towards the end of their stay the brigade, with its accompanying Argylls, put on a ceremonial parade. It was a scintillating performance that drew words of warm approval from the inspecting officer, their host the Duke. He gave them a polished little speech about their impressive standards of skill on the beaches, of endurance among the hills, and of turnout and discipline on parade. He wished them everything good for the future.

The brigade commander moved to the next part of the ritual. He removed his cap and called for three cheers for the Duke of Argyll.

In the brief pause before the first 'Hip, hip', a stern, defiant voice came from the ranks of the Argylls.

'MacDonalds, stand fast,' ordered a senior NCO bleakly.

They did.

THE WOOD FOR THE TREES

As a matter of both courtesy and policy, Lieutenant Colonel Durnford-Slater of No. 3 Commando made a point of calling upon the owners of large holdings of land when his unit moved to a new area in Britain. It reduced friction. Troops who were exercising constantly in cross-country movement were bound to leave some traces of their passing, however well disciplined they were. Untidiness could be put right and damage to crops and livestock minimized by a sensible liaison.

Lord Glasgow was a Scottish landowner who was gratified by the colonel's thoughtfulness. He gave his visitor a drink and showed him around his estate. The conversation turned easily from training requirements to the difficulties caused to agriculture and silviculture by wartime manpower shortages, and specifically to a large, dying tree.

The tree was sited on a narrow ride between two plantations of young saplings. It must clearly be brought down in an organized manner before old age and a high wind collapsed it. The problem was to fell it without its harming some of the saplings when it came to earth. This task required skills beyond those of the few remaining employees of Lord Glasgow not currently serving in His Majesty's forces.

Colonel Durnford-Slater volunteered a proposed solution. Blowing things up, he said, was a thing his soldiers were good at. It was a highly skilled business. His demolition experts could sever the tree trunk with a nicely calculated charge and bring it down precisely where they wanted it, which in this case would be along the ride well clear of the young plantation.

Lord Glasgow accepted this offer with gratitude and enthusiasm. The timing of the job was discussed over a further drink. The project began to acquire something of a ceremonial ingredient. Mightn't it be a good idea if Lord Glasgow first gave luncheon to Colonel Durnford-Slater and his officers, prior to their all going together to view the tree-felling? The colonel thought this a delightful concept and accepted with many thanks.

The lunch was a great success, distinguished by goodwill and merriment. The demolition officer missed it. He was busy preparing and laying his charge, having been urged by his commanding officer to take absolutely no chances on there being a mistake. After all this hospitality build-up, it would be pretty embarrassing if there were no more than a loud pop on the trunk of an immobile tree. The demolitions officer had been reassuring. He had done his sums with care, had rechecked them, and had re-rechecked the recheck.

The lunch over, Lord Glasgow led his guests from his house, along a winding path through a wood, to the young plantation and the doomed, dying tree. They stood in an informal group on a low rise. The colonel spoke briefly to his host about the advances in explosive technology stimulated by the war, and nodded to the demolitions officer.

The demolitions officer, already crouched over his box, hands gripping the T-bar of the plunger, pressed down hard.

There was an immense, deafening detonation. The tree disintegrated into countless parts of varying size. These, accompanied by an impressive tonnage of earth, rock and undergrowth, rose upwards and outwards, hovered cloudily, and crashed at random throughout the plantation, destroying several hundred saplings as they did so.

The demolitions officer was the first to break the subsequent silence. He had been examining some figures pencilled on to the back of an envelope.

'I see,' he said helpfully, 'I put the decimal point in the wrong place.'

Lord Glasgow led his guests out of the wood. Nobody spoke. They closed wordlessly around him once, when he paused at a bend in the track from which his house came into view. All the windows had been blown in.

Emotion overcame him at his front door. He was not a man to show weakness publicly. He shut himself in the downstairs lavatory until his composure had been regained. Ready once more to face the world, he pulled the chain, as simulated evidence that his purpose had been to do with natural functions and not with self-pity.

The cistern came away with the chain and fell on his head.

CENSUS RETURN

WHETHER the reason was scepticism about their cause, leadership, weaponry, equipment, prospects or some of everything listed, the Italian Army in the Western Desert showed modified enthusiasm for their task as 1940 moved into 1941.

Their artillerymen were much respected by their British, Indian and Australian opponents. The rest had a leaning towards what a later generation would call unilateral disarmament. This practice could promote situations demanding initiative and improvisation.

A pioneer confronter of a surrender problem was a subaltern of the 11th Hussars, out ahead with a troop of armoured cars in the early days of the first entirely successful British offensive of the Second World War.

There was mention of a modest collection of prisoners among the first of his wirelessed reports. He had, he said, taken five.

His next message raised the total to fourteen.

An hour later he had ninety-three and was beginning to wonder what to do with them.

As time passed he became less precise in his head count. He passed on successive bulletins of 'about two hundred', 'about five hundred', 'about a thousand'.

By the late afternoon he had switched to a fresh basis of calculation. 'I now have with me,' he signalled, 'two and a half acres of prisoners.'

THE MOUNTAINS OF MATILDA

An Irish officer of the Royal Artillery who went into a Cairo nightclub on Saint Patrick's Day in 1942 was gratified by the music being played. The band was giving a rendering of a recognizable version of 'The Mountains of Mourne'. It was a work with which he had assumed them to be unfamiliar.

He identified the band's tutor as Captain Blair Mayne of the Royal Ulster Rifles and the Special Air Service. In more peaceable times Captain Mayne had been an Irish rugby international, had represented the Lions in South Africa, and was a heavyweight boxer of note. His manner was persuasive.*

He invited the gunner to join his table. The table was heavily supplied with bottles and was attended by seven other Irish officers, all singing 'The Mountains of Mourne'. At the end of the last verse the drummer rat-tat-tatted and the bandleader bowed elegantly to Captain Mayne. What, he asked, would the captain like next? The captain said that he would like 'The Mountains of Mourne' and he would like it now. The band met his wishes.

After the fifteenth performance of 'The Mountains of Mourne', various English, Scottish, Welsh, New Zealand, South African, Polish and Free French patrons, who had

---

* By the end of the war he had been awarded the DSO with three bars and had destroyed more aircraft, German and Italian, on the ground than had any allied fighter pilot in the air. Unsubstantiated but convincing rumour had it that he was once due to have been decorated with the Victoria Cross. The recommendation was cancelled after he felled his commanding officer during a discussion about discipline.

73

''E SWORE BACK AT ME, SIR'

earlier applauded and in some cases participated, began to
show signs of dissatisfaction. They favoured cultural variety,
they said. What about a change to something really good like
'Begin the Beguine' or 'A Nightingale Sang in Berkeley
Square'?

They put these recommendations to the bandleader. He
referred them to the Irish table. Members of the table suggested that consultation with Captain Mayne would be nice.
Captain Mayne was quietly adamant. It was, he explained,
Saint Patrick's Day. He would like the band to continue to
play 'The Mountains of Mourne'.

74

Satiated with Paddy Mayne's favourite nostalgic ditty, a high proportion of the customers moved on elsewhere. The resentment of the survivors was amplified by the arrival of six Australian officers, dedicated choristers all. Captain Mayne taught them the words of 'The Mountains of Mourne'. They were keen students.

The gunner had by now lost count, but at the end of what must have been something like the thirtieth encore he went to the gents. As he left the table, a debate was in its early stages. This 'Mountains of Mourne' stuff was okay so far as it went, the Australians were arguing, but it was possible to have too much of a good thing. Why not ring the changes a bit? What about 'Waltzing Matilda', for example?

When the gunner returned from the gents the band was playing 'The Mountains of Mourne'. Paddy Mayne sucked his knuckles between verses. The six Australians, prostrate, were recovering consciousness.

Later the gunner moved on to another appointment. Later still he returned to the nightclub for a last drink. Departing guests tried to dissuade him from entering.

'I wouldn't go in there,' they said. 'The band only knows one bloody tune.'

' "The Mountains of Mourne?" '

'No. "Waltzing Matilda". There's some Irish looney and a bunch of Aussies singing it. Over and over again. They've been at it for hours.'

The gunner looked at his watch. Saint Patrick's Day had ended two hours previously.

SYMPATHETIC DETONATION

WITHIN a short time of the evacuation of the British Expeditionary Force from Dunkirk in 1940, and after Fighter Command of the Royal Air Force had broken in the Battle of Britain whatever hopes the Germans seriously held of mounting a seaborne invasion of the British Isles, the Chiefs of Staff ordered that a study be made of the resources that would be needed to land again in continental Europe.

The study, codenamed Skyscraper, was entrusted to General Sir Bernard Paget, the Commander in Chief Home Forces, and his staff. They were thorough about it. They were dealing with long-term aspirations, not early prospects. They sensibly took their time, assembling useful data as it became available. It was not until the end of 1941, when the United States had become embroiled in the war, that provisional planning began to connect with reality.

General Paget's planners concluded that five airborne divisions would, among much complicated more, be necessary. General Paget examined this recommended *sine qua non* with a critical eye, agreed that it was indeed essential, and moved his thinking to the next logical steps. Relative manpower strengths suggested that three of the airborne divisions might be American and two British. To expand the existing small British airborne force to two divisions would require an extensive programme of recruitment and training. Training, and subsequent operations, would be impossible without an adequate supply of suitable aircraft.

All existing types of aircraft from which parachutists could jump, or by which gliders could be towed, were under the control of Air Marshal Sir Arthur Harris, the Air Officer Commanding Bomber Command. General Paget went to see him.

Bomber Harris was a man of strong convictions. He was uncompromising in their expression. He knew precisely how to win the war. All this land-fighting business was irrelevant and outdated. The thing to do was to drop bombs on Germany. If only everyone would stop chasing will-o'-the-wisps up blind alleys, recognize a panacea when they saw one, and generally get their emotions under control, a bit of common-sense would be injected into the conduct of the war.

The Harris scheme demanded few concessions from doubters. All that they had to do was agree to a reasonable reduction of the Navy and of the Army to a sort of Home Guard, and to the diversion of industrial and human effort to where any fool could see that it mattered, the design, production and manning of aeroplanes, well supplied with bigger and better bombs.

The Paget–Harris discussion did not prosper. Harris listened impatiently until he had discovered what he was being got at about, and then put his finger on what he considered to be a self-evident flaw in the Paget concept.

Parachutists and glider-borne troops were useless, he said. They didn't explode when they hit the ground.

SHADES OF GREYS

ONE of the casualties of some heavy and confused fighting in Italy in 1943 was a trooper of the Royal Scots Greys. These cavalrymen of distinguished lineage had long since been converted to armour. They were commanded by Lieutenant Colonel Twisleton-Wykeham-Fiennes.

The trooper's tank had been brewed up by a German 88. He had got out with difficulty and removed himself to the nearest cover. The shifting state of the battle left him out of luck. He was overrun by German infantry and taken away as a prisoner.

The Germans, as was their custom with most of those of their captured opponents whom they regarded as possessing ethnic respectability, treated him as well as prevailing conditions allowed. They gave him water and a piece of black bread, and accepted him companionably as a sharer of their holes in the ground when concentrations of shelling and mortar fire from his friends came too close. During an interval of relative calm, he was escorted rearwards and delivered to a Panzer intelligence officer.

The trooper was equipped by both training and temperament to withstand the blandishments of interrogators seeking information. He had been taught repeatedly that the Geneva Convention required him to disclose to his captors no more than his name, rank and number. He did not find this restriction onerous. He was not by nature of a chatty disposition.

The Panzer intelligencer, genial and persuasive, spoke

78

nearly faultless English. He welcomed the trooper courteously, offered him a cigarette and a huge slug of Italian brandy, and congratulated him on getting out of his burning tank unwounded. He hoped that the trooper had not incurred too many painful scratches and abrasions whilst subsequently crawling to safety.

The trooper ignored the brandy, took the cigarette and gave his name, rank and number.

The intelligence officer became discursive about the good old days in the Western Desert. Warfare in a vast, barren arena, uncluttered by civilians, had been exciting and honourable. He himself had fought against the Scots Greys on a number of occasions. He had the greatest admiration for them. Had the trooper been in the Desert?

The trooper, who had, said nothing.

The intelligencer moved slickly to more recent occurrences. His respect for the regiment remained undiminished, he said, but they shared a weakness with most British units. Their radio security was, to put it bluntly, lousy. Did the trooper agree?

The trooper, who did, said nothing.

What these free-flowing conversationalists seemed not to have absorbed, said the intelligencer, was that the Germans operated an extraordinarily efficient tactical radio interception set-up. From this, and from various other sources which he wouldn't elaborate upon at the moment, he had assembled an almost complete picture of the command structure of the Scots Greys.

The trooper, who wasn't surprised, said nothing.

The intelligencer picked up some papers, neatly clipped together. In case his guest thought he was exaggerating, he said, it might be helpful to name names. He then read out an almost complete nominal roll that included the second in command, all the squadron commanders, most of the troop commanders, the adjutant, and the regimental sergeant major.

At the end of this offering he apologized charmingly for his remissness in letting his official duties override his responsibilities as a host. He pushed the brandy forward again and offered another cigarette.

The trooper left the brandy where it was and lit the cigarette. He had never been a man to confuse taciturnity with bad manners. This sort of hospitality, he felt, deserved acknowledgement. Continued silence would be churlish. He repeated his name, rank and number.

The intelligencer drew on his own cigarette, sat back and became confidential. The trooper would have noticed, he remarked, that, despite the comprehensive accuracy of the list of names that had been read out, there was an important omission. The commanding officer had not been mentioned. It was about this gap in their knowledge that he and his colleagues would value his new friend's advice.

There had, frankly, been differences of opinion in German intelligence circles about the identity of this colonel of tanks. He had originally been recorded under the name of Twisleton. He seemed later to have been replaced by someone called Wykeham. But no sooner had Wykeham been logged in on the order of battle than Twisleton was back. Any facile idea that Wykeham had been a *locum tenens*, looking after things while Twisleton was on leave or recovering from wounds, had been dissipated by later evidence that both Twisleton and Wykeham had been at work simultaneously, either in alternation or in tandem. Consideration of this interesting experiment in command technique had been clouded by the insertion of somebody named Fiennes, which no German could either spell or pronounce. Fiennes was obviously enmeshed with the first two, with whom for many purposes he appeared to be interchangeable.

After much thought and discussion, and the discarding of a number of farfetched hypotheses, the problem had been narrowed down to something manageable. Current argument ranged over three possible solutions: (a) the Scots Greys were commanded by a committee; (b) the regiment's RT discipline was more effective than had previously been believed. The use on the air of multiple aliases was undoubtedly confusing to their opponents; or (c) there was no such persons as Twisleton, Wykeham and Fiennes. The names were a front to mask the anonymity of an ingenious leader who was thought to be planning some unpleasant masterstroke.

Would the prisoner, after first please helping himself to another cigarette and if he so wished getting stuck into the brandy, care to comment?

The trooper lit up thoughtfully and considered the matter. He concluded that a truthful reply could bring no comfort to the enemy. 'If you're talking about the colonel,' he said laconically, 'I've never been able to work out what his name is either.'

ROLL UP YOUR SLEEVES

THE anopheles mosquito breeds in stagnant water. One of its preferred forms of nourishment is human blood. It settles on exposed skin, inserts a probe and sucks. When it feels replete it goes away. The blood donor gets malaria.

A multiplication of this simple process once destroyed a Roman army in Sicily. About two thousand years later, the total battle casualties inflicted by the Japanese on the 14th Army in Burma were one third of the number of troops put out of action by the anopheles mosquito.

A daily compulsory consumption of mepachrine tablets, taken under supervision and with names ticked off on lists by NCOs, reduced this attrition. Supplementary measures were based on the need for potential victims to expose as little skin as possible and on the mosquitoes' preference for operating by night. It became a disciplinary offence for a soldier of whatever rank to fail to roll down his sleeves, or not to wear slacks instead of shorts after dusk.

Those who objected to being told how to dress when off duty, or who genuinely felt more comfortable with their sleeves rolled up, or who liked to think that the exposure of a stretch of manly, sun-bronzed torso enhanced their prospects with the ladies, were out of luck. The military police were remorseless, particularly in training and recreation areas in India. 'Sleeves up, run 'em in' became a catchphrase with them, an obsession.

One of their catches in Calcutta was a dissolute prewar regular private soldier who, even by his own exacting standards, had rather overstretched himself. His company commander examined the charge sheet with respect: breaking out of camp; absence without leave; drunk and disorderly; being in an out-of-bounds area; destruction of a male urinal at a railway station; insulting remarks to a superior officer; resisting arrest; assaulting three military policemen . . . it went on and on.

The outcome, a remand for CO's orders followed by a stretch in a detention barracks, was inevitable. The due processes of law must first be honoured.

'March him in, Sar'n't Major.'

The accused, as was his custom on these familiar occasions, was elegantly turned out from his immaculately shaven face to the gleaming toecaps of his boots. He stood motionless and expressionless as the CSM read out the endless list of offences, allowing himself an occasional twitch of the mouth when he heard in reminiscent pleasure an account of one of his more sensational outrages into official jargon.

'Anything to say?'

'Nossir.'

'First witness.'

This was a sergeant of the military police. He stamped into the company office, saluted quiveringly, and delivered his evidence in a piercing, high-decibel, near shriek.

'*Sir*,' he bellowed, 'at nineteen hundred hours on seven February I received information that the accused was in a certain house in the out-of-bounds area, *sir*. I proceeded there without delay. The lady in charge, on being consulted, directed me to room number fourteen. The door was locked. I hammered on it and said, "I know you are there open this door at once." The accused replied that he would not do so.'

The company commander here interrupted in the interests of historical accuracy. He could well believe that the accused would refuse to open a door in a brothel when instructed to do so by a military policeman, but it seemed inherently unlikely that the terms in which the refusal had been framed had been anything as prosaic as 'I will not do so'.

Sergeant-Major (lecturing the young officers of a new battalion of an old regiment):
'YOU 'AVEN'T GOT TO MAKE TRADITIONS, YOU'VE ONLY GOT TO KEEP 'EM. YOU
WAS THE BLANKSHIRE REGIMENT IN 1810. YOU ARE THE BLANKSHIRE
REGIMENT IN 1916. NEVER MORE CLEARLY 'AS 'ISTORY REPEATED ITSELF'

'What were his exact words?'

'He said, *sir*,' bawled the sergeant, offended, ' "piss off, you
redcap sod. Go and fight some Japs for a change." '

'Oh, I see,' said the company commander. This was more
authentic-sounding material but he wondered whether he had
been wise to raise the issue.

'Then?' he said.

'I broke down the door, *sir*. Accused was lying on a bed,
naked. He had two women with him, one on either side. They
were nood too. I at once said, "I suppose you realize you are
contravening the anti-malarial regulations." '

FRANKLY SPEAKING

TOWARDS the end of 1942, General Mark Clark of the United States Army, accompanied by a French-speaking British officer of the Special Boat Section, went on a reconnaissance to French North Africa. Participation by generals in two-men reconnaissances far ahead of their main forces is rare. The circumstances were exceptional.

The German Afrika Korps had been beaten decisively at El Alamein in October and were retreating westwards. Their withdrawal was skilfully conducted, and they were still dangerous in the delaying battles they fought, but their hopes of recovery were slight. The Allied intention was to reduce the hopes from slight to nothing by amphibious landings well behind them.

A large force, part British, part American, was to go ashore at a selection of places in Tunisia, Algeria and Morocco. All three were French colonial possessions, controlled by the Vichy government which had ordered French affairs since the French capitulation to Germany in 1940. It was of central importance to the Anglo-American planners to get an authoritative assessment of whether the French commanders on the spot would oppose the landings vigorously, or would desist from interference, perhaps after token opposition to safeguard honour.

Only a very senior officer could undertake this task. An American would be more acceptable than a British general. The French had not forgiven the destruction of their fleet by the Royal Navy at Oran in 1940. General Clark was accordingly dispatched on his unusual mission.

He went by British submarine. Her voyage was uneventful, her landfall accurate. Clark and his SBS interpreter–escort transferred to a folboat, had a wet, bumpy ride in the starlit night, and waded on to the North African shore.

The local harbourmaster had been recommended by Intelligence as the contact man to head for. He was, they said, sympathetic to the Allies, reliable and discreet. He should be able to put them in touch with the people Clark wanted to see.

They set out in search of him. Before they had gone far, a voice called softly to them from beside the track they were following. They froze. Then they eased themselves slowly to the ground and silently slid forward the safety catches of their Tommy guns.

A small boy, dressed in what in the diffused starlight looked like a ragged white nightshirt, stepped unselfconsciously towards them. He examined them appraisingly, and made an offer in French. 'You want my sister?' he asked.

'No,' said the SBS officer.

The boy took this rejection without rancour. 'What about my brother?' he suggested. 'Very clean. But more expensive.'

The SBS officer declined him too. General Clark became impatient and demanded a translation. He was given one. It did not please him but he identified a means of cutting a corner.

'The kid's harmless,' said the general. 'We can use him as a guide. Tell him I want the harbourmaster.'

The SBS officer put the general's wishes into French.

The boy thought it over. 'It should be all right,' he said at last, 'but he'll cost at least twice as much as my brother.'

NUN SO FAIR

THE vows of the sisters in the enclosed order included one of silence, in addition to the customary pledges to poverty, chastity and obedience. Because of the silence, the motives of the Mother Superior in succouring Lance Corporal Urquhart of the Essex Scottish were never fully clear to him.

They were, in fact, first, Christian compassion, the acceptance of an obligation to tend the sick and the halt and, second, remembrance of her father and three brothers, killed on the Aisne and at Verdun over twenty years earlier. She had forgiven the Germans who had destroyed all the menfolk of her family. She saw no reason to let forgiveness interfere with her duty to aid the Germans' present enemies.

Urquhart had been in the 2nd Canadian Division, destroyed in the shambles of the Dieppe raid in August 1942. He had been hit by a shell fragment in the fleshy part of the thigh and had been left behind with most of his battalion, alive and dead, when the last landing and support craft withdrew from behind the smokescreen at the end of a calamitous day.

Abetted by a medical orderly, he had pretended that his wound was worse than it was. He slipped away by night from a crowded dressing station. His boyhood in Saskatchewan had equipped him handsomely with the skills needed to travel unobtrusively across country. He moved at night and laid up by day, in woods mostly, once under the hay in a barn and, less comfortably, in a culvert. He fed himself on carefully rationed bits of his emergency ration plain chocolate, and on stolen eggs and unripe fruit. Once he milked a lonely cow. His

87

immediate aim was to get as far as possible from Dieppe. He would work out an ultimate destination when he was at least fifty miles from the Channel coast.

On the sixth day his wound went bad. Pain was joined by a high fever. He crawled, through a palpitating red mist, from an orchard in which he had been sheltering towards a vegetable garden. He fainted. He awoke between coarse white sheets in a small, cool, clean room with a crucifix on the wall.

A middle-aged nun sat on a wooden chair beside his bed. She smiled, took his temperature, gave him some refreshingly cool apple juice, and tinkered professionally with the fresh bandaging around his thigh. Then she changed his sweat-soaked sheets. She said nothing. He fell asleep once more.

On the following morning the Mother Superior came to see him. She was charming, cheerful, and her English was serviceable if hesitant. The nuns, she said, would look after him until he was fully recovered. Friends, she added mysteriously, would then help him to 'go home'.

There was an important domestic point that he should know. The nuns would see to his needs. But they would not speak. She herself was authorized to speak only on essential matters, as now. She smiled, and left him.

The sisters were superb nurses, kindly and efficient. Four days after the Mother Superior's visit, he was able to get shakily out of bed. Five days after that he began a programme of loosening-up exercises. He progressed to press-ups, knee-bends, running on the spot, and shadow boxing. Two weeks later still he felt fit to travel. He asked if he could see the Reverend Mother again.

She seemed sad when she arrived. He asked about her friends who might help him. They were the cause of the sadness. On the previous night the Gestapo had made extensive arrests. Most of her friends were included. Others would replace them and rebuild the organization, but it would take time. Meanwhile he must stay hidden in the convent.

Urquhart at once recognized the risk she would run. He said no, he would leave at once, alone, that night. After long argument, she dissuaded him. Even the Germans would not break into the convent of an enclosed order of nuns. He must stay quiet, be patient and wait. God would be good to him. The sisters prayed daily for him.

During the next month Urquhart thought that he would go mad. He was young and at a peak of good health. He was confined to a small cell. Saintly but silent nuns brought his food. The only books that they lent him were in French, which he did not read. He did his exercises. There was nobody to talk to, nothing to read, little tangible to look forward to. He wanted, above all, fresh air, a chance to stretch his legs, freedom.

The Mother Superior could have been a clairvoyant. She walked into his cell one day, smiling, grinning almost, carrying a cloth bundle. 'Put this on over your clothes,' she said.

Urquhart did. He wriggled about to let things fall into place, she made some minor tucks and adjustments, and to external viewers he was a nun.

She took him to see himself in a wall mirror. He laughed. She giggled, and told him to fold his arms and tuck his hands up his sleeves. She gave him a last careful examination and giggled again. 'You'll pass at a distance,' she said. 'You can have one hour a day in the rose garden. Remember, nobody talks. If I come out and nod to you, walk *slowly* away, back to your cell.'

Life improved immeasurably for Urquhart. He awoke daily with an intense anticipatory pleasure, his hour of freedom ahead of him. He was never alone in the rose garden. Wordless sisters paced meditatively up and down reading devotional works, saying their rosaries to themselves. He shuffled demurely in their wake, thinking over a scheme to head for Spain when the Reverend Mother's reconstituted organization of friends was ready for him.

Most of the nuns were getting on in life. He glanced at them briefly from time to time with friendly indifference. But there was one, young, fresh-complexioned, whom he began to study furtively with increasing absorption. Even her tent-like robes did not hide the natural grace and litheness of her movements. Each day Urquhart looked for her. If she was late, he became impatient, disappointed, almost desolate. He felt a strange delight when she did arrive.

It came to him with a high clarity early one morning that he was no longer simply pondering on the joys to come of his hour in the rose garden. It was the garden *with her in it*. Urquhart knew what that meant. He was in love. He, a Canadian infantry corporal disguised absurdly as a nun, on the run from Germans who would shoot or imprison him if they identified him, was in love with a beautiful girl pledged to chastity and silence, not counting poverty and obedience, which were not altogether relevant to his condition.

Commonsense suggested that, with all these obstacles to clear, the best thing he could do was forget about it. Commonsense has little to do with love. Urquhart dreamed besotted, romantic, impossible dreams. There was nothing he could do about them, apart from dream them. He paced the garden in his daily hour of liberty, gazing longingly under his wimple at his willowy beloved.

Then, one morning, the numbers in the rose garden began imperceptibly to thin. First one ageing nun, then another, left on unguessed-at errands. Urquhart, seven minutes left before he was due back in his cell, was alone with her.

He was filled with a huge, nervous joy. He abandoned covert glances for a bold stare. She stared back. Their eyes met, held. The makings of a smile twitched her lips. Then she *winked*.

Urquhart lost control. He took his hands from his sleeves, strode forward and embraced her.

'Let go, you stupid bugger,' she said. 'Wiggins, Beds and Herts. I've been in the bloody place since Dunkirk.'

DEATH OR GLORY OR PERHAPS NOT

MAJOR General Orde Wingate, the Chindit commander, was an almost mesmeric speaker who put over a harsh message.

Other generals dealt oratorically from time to time in formulas adapted from Mr Winston Churchill's forecast of blood and sweat and toil and tears but, like Mr Churchill, they were apt to describe these disabilities as necessary present payment for future good.

Wingate, when addressing his troops, left out the second part of the message. He stayed firmly with the blood and tears, with a generous measure of death added as subsidiary encouragement. To those who never heard him it seems unbelievable that exhortations of this sort could inspire British soldiers to fight harder. Those who did hear him say that it usually worked.

Consumer resistance was not entirely unknown. A conspicuous example came from the Cameronians, recruited largely in Glasgow from rhetoric-proof cynics.

One of Wingate's calls to valour and sacrifice came to its dramatic climax when he stared hypnotically at the nearest rifleman and said slowly, 'You are going to die in Burma.'

'In that case,' said the rifleman reasonably, 'I'm not bloody well going there.'

INNER CIRCLE

THE theory of long-range penetration, as devised, refined and practised in Burma in 1943 and 1944, was an adaptation of guerrilla warfare principles of long standing.

The Burma version, which led to much controversy, involved the insertion of infantry columns into deep jungle, well behind the Japanese forward positions, charged with disrupting Japanese communications and supply arrangements. The columns were to be resupplied by air and their operations coordinated by wireless.

The first Chindit expedition, of brigade strength, went in and came out on foot in 1943. Its practical achievements were meagre; its moral effect remarkable.

The second, in 1944, was a much more elaborate affair. The bulk of the troops entered by glider, or by transport aircraft landing on improvised airstrips. Major General Orde Wingate, the prophet and progenitor of long-range penetration, was killed early on when his aircraft crashed. The strategic picture was altered by a major Japanese attack in the forward area. The Chindits were largely diverted into doing things, at a heavy cost, not included in the Wingate concept.

The controversy resolved around complaints from critics that the whole thing had got out of hand. Long-range penetration, it was argued, when properly conducted on a reasonable scale, could provide useful ancillary help to the only operations that could be decisive; those of the main force. When an over abundance of people and material were put into a fancy organization for guerrilla soldiering, the result could only be an expensive and irrelevant diversion of resources from where they were needed.

The purity of the argument was heavily clouded by the personality of Wingate. To some he was a messianic genius. To others an obsessed charlatan. To all he was abrasive, moody, offensive, eccentric, and utterly contemptuous of those who disagreed with him.

As has been customary down the ages, the soldiers who actually did the work were unaware that there was discord among the policy makers, and would not have cared much if they had known. Their preoccupations were local and domestic.

There was the physical strain of marching day after day through hilly jungle, carrying weapons, ammunition and, in packs on their backs, everything they needed for sustenance and night-time warmth. There was the strict march discipline necessary to conceal the traces of their passing. If a wireless set went on the blink, or was damaged by accident or in action, there would be no food because the air suppliers could not be told where to drop it. And, of course, there was the usual risk run by soldiers of being killed or wounded while fighting.

It was the second component of this last risk that was the most daunting. In conventional forms of warfare the wounded might run out of luck but they had at least a fair prospect of being recovered, given immediate elementary treatment and being removed to a hospital. In the second Chindit operation, many benefited from a variant of this process through the agency of dedicated American pilots who flew out casualties in light aircraft. In the 1943 operation the option did not exist.

Then, the badly wounded and the badly sick had to be abandoned. Columns with tasks to perform, and with the survival of the majority at stake, could not have their movements constricted by people incapable of marching. The patients were given such small comforts in the way of food, water and drugs as was available, and were left to their own

93

devices and to the mercies of the Japanese. The Japanese were not merciful.

Six weeks after the fragmented survivors of the 1943 expedition had made their way in small parties back to India, undernourished, exhausted and many of them diseased, a ragged-looking Gurkha soldier presented himself cautiously to an outpost of an Indian battalion manning a forward British position in Assam. He was identified as friendly, welcomed, fed, and sent to the rear.

There he was fed further, interrogated, deloused, put into hospital for treatment and observation, released when declared fit to travel, and sent on the long journey to rejoin his parent unit. He underwent all these processes philosophically, but was entirely adamant on one point. He refused to be parted from his map, a sweat-stained paper, badly frayed at its folds.

His reappearance at his battalion stimulated unaffected pleasure. They had last seen him when they left him under a tree, ten miles from the Chindwin river, with a crippling leg wound. They had on that occasion given him food, field dressings, disinfectant, and heartfelt good wishes, privately not laced with optimism.

He had, he said, crawled farther into the jungle after their departure and had stayed hidden for several days, frugally rationing his food. He had been pleased to find that his wound was slowly mending. He could at first hobble, and then limp. On the twelfth day he decided to limp the 150 miles or so back to India.

He gave a casually laconic account of this undertaking, which to him seemed an obvious and normal thing to do. Patient questioning drew from him reluctant details of how he supplemented what was left of his food by helping himself to a little rice that had been left in an abandoned Burman village and, once, by stealing a chicken from an unabandoned Burman village.

Both when moving and lying up, he had exercised all the

precautions in which he had been trained. He had only twice seen Japanese and had had no difficulty in evading them. His arrival at the Indian battalion's outpost had caused him no surprise. After all, he had had his map to guide him.

The frayed map, which he handed over for inspection, was much admired, partly because it had shared his adventures and partly because it was a diagrammatic representation of the layout of the London underground railway system.

COME BACK TO ERIN

L ANCE Corporal Mangan, who in 1941 had been posted as a deserter from an Irish regiment in the British Army, presented himself at the regimental depot in Northern Ireland in 1944. He had not so much come to give himself up, he explained, as to describe what had happened to him. He was anxious to get back to work without delay.

Whilst on leave in Dublin he had been unwise enough to talk knowledgeably in a pub about his aptitude in the use of the Bren gun, the No. 4 rifle, the 2-inch mortar and other contemporary weaponry. His expertise had provoked much admiration, which had been expressed in a practical form by the provision of constant refills for his glass. When he awoke he was in a strange room. He felt unwell and his hands were roped together behind his back.

It was pointed out to him that his trained skills with small arms would make him a valuable asset to the Irish Republican Army. He had been nominated as a weapon training instructor. All he had to do was to give lessons. Failure to cooperate would lead to the death of his old mother.

Mangan cooperated for more than three years. He was at first kept under guard in an isolated cottage in the country. Later, when it was clear that he was fully compromised and that he was so devoted to his mother that he would do anything to spare her from harm, he was let out on a sort of ticket of leave. He reported himself to his controllers at weekly intervals and from time to time was taken away blindfolded to an unidentifiable place to give his lessons. This regime had prevailed until the previous week when his mother had been run over by a tram. Mangan had returned to regimental duty immediately after the funeral.

A court martial was mandatory. By the nature of Mangan's misadventures, witnesses were sparse. His kidnappers were, to put it at its lowest, unlikely to offer evidence. The government of the Irish Free State, a neutral country, could hardly be asked for comment on the credibility of a statement made before a military tribunal convened by a belligerent power in whose armed forces an Irish citizen had voluntarily enlisted. Mangan was acquitted of the charge of desertion. The court offered him its sympathies on the loss of his mother and spoke appreciatively of his resourcefulness and determination in rejoining his regiment at the first reasonable opportunity. Mangan became a minor hero. The Ministry of Information put out a short piece about him. Strangers bought him drinks.

At the following week's pay parade, Mangan pointed out respectfully that there seemed to have been something of a mistake. He had been given one week's pay. As he understood it, because his long absence had been no fault of his and had been certified as involuntary by the verdict of the court martial, he had all the time been on the regimental books. His position was analogous to that of a prisoner-of-war. He was owed not one week's pay but three years and seven months' pay.

The justice of this claim was indisputable. The mechanics of meeting it took a little while to arrange. Three weeks later Mangan was paid in full.

He deserted again the same night and bought a small farm in County Wicklow. His mother kept house for him.

BALKAN SHOWER

THE Gulf of Kotor in Montenegro is a deep fjord of spectacular beauty backed by steeply rising limestone mountains. In present time it attracts a multitude of tourists from all over Europe. In the winter of 1944 its visitors were less pacific. Advanced elements of the German 21st Mountain Corps were using the coast road from the south in an attempt to break out of the Balkans before the exits at the top of the peninsula were sealed by the advancing Russians and possibly the British from Italy.

At Risan, a small coastal town at the head of one of the inlets on the gulf, the Germans were stopped by two brigades of Marshal Tito's partisans. With the partisans was a British battery of 25-pounder guns of the Royal Artillery. Local defence of the gun positions was the task of a troop of No. 43 Royal Marine Commando.

Fighting was extensive and bloody. Partisan and German casualties were heavy. The guns were supreme. The Germans withdrew to try to make their way out by a route farther inland. The battle over, the British, to whom the Yugoslavs had offered no part in the pursuit, concentrated upon cleaning themselves up.

To the gunners this posed few problems. Because of the requirements of their trade, every man travelled on wheels. There was adequate room in the transport for spare clothing, bedding and personal possessions. There was an adaptable and well-equipped pool of technicians capable of devising a variety of construction work and plumbing from unpromising materials. In the ruined upland village of Bileca they impro-

98

vised a rudimentary hot shower in which they soaped themselves and soaked with gratification. When they had cleansed
themselves satisfactorily, the battery commander, who had
rightly given priority to his own followers, offered the hospitality of the showers to his commando escort.

The marines were in much worse hygienic condition than
were the gunners. The commando scale of equipment was
designed to cover the personal needs of a man on an operation
lasting for a maximum of forty-eight hours. For six weeks the
marines had marched over miles of mountainous country, had
been drenched by violent rainstorms, and had slept wearing
the only set of clothes they possessed on the earth floors of
peasant cottages and livestock lean-tos. They shaved daily,
washed the grime from their faces, and kept their weapons
clean. Otherwise they were filthy. Some were literally lousy.

Their troop commander was Captain Bob Loudoun. When
the offer of the use of the shower was put to him, he decided to
give himself a rare luxury. He had raised, trained and
cherished his troop. He had led it in action from the Anzio
beachhead to Montenegro and had been wounded at its head
in the Dalmatian islands. He was immensely proud of his men
and he took a fatherly care over their wellbeing. He would
personally see to it that every one of them would wallow in the
steam and soap and wash away the muck of weeks. In the
meantime he would cheat.

He would start things off by taking a private shower; a
prolonged, hedonistic, luxurious soaping and sluicing in limit-
less warm, running water whilst he thought his own undis-
tracted thoughts, temporarily undisturbed by responsibility
and concern for the followers he honoured above all men. He
ordered one of his subalterns to take the troop out on a
training exercise. When they returned, sweatier and dirtier
than ever, they would be met by a glowing, scrubbed Loudoun, who would tell them proudly of the marvellous surprise
that awaited them.

He allowed ten minutes for them to get well clear of the
wrecked village. Then he rolled his towel neatly, tucked it
under his arm, and walked briskly, humming to himself, to the

'A FINE BODY OF MEN, COLONEL!'

gunners' headquarters. The gunner sentry came smartly to attention, sloped arms, and smacked the open palm of his right hand against the butt of his rifle in salute.

'Good morning,' said Bob Loudoun, returning the salute.

'Morning, sir,' said the sentry.

'Where's the shower?' asked Loudoun keenly.

'They've just gone out on a training exercise,' said the sentry.

100

NOSE FOR DIRECTION

COKE was short and broad and strong. An uncomplicated and helpful man, from kindness of heart and an inability to be happy unless physically occupied, he voluntarily did all sorts of little things to ease the daily lives of his companions. Coke, whistling out of tune, put the disinfectant in the pit latrines, unloaded more than his due share of supplies from vehicles and took over the carrying of the Bren towards the end of cross-country marches.

Every military organization is better and happier for the presence of someone like Coke. In his case, the beneficiaries were a commando troop in the Mediterranean.

But, like many a fighting man before and since, the hardworking, enduring, uncomplaining, good-hearted Coke had a weakness. Achilles, had he served in Coke's time, would have had to be excused boots. Napoleon's haemorrhoids are believed to have influenced the outcome of Waterloo. The interpretation of the orders of General Ulysses S. Grant was a matter for careful calculation by his staff, who had first to make a fine judgement of how sober he was when he issued them.

Coke's problem led to no strategic complications. It was local. On the not very frequent occasions when Coke had a drink or two, he would pick a fight. He chose his opponents not by the degree of offence they had given but by the simpler criterion of size. Coke's idea of an interesting evening out was to get his alcohol–bloodstream ratio properly adjusted, approach the largest man he could find, and insult him.

Not surprisingly, Coke always lost. These failures did not dispirit him.

A crisp bout with a former All Black Rugby forward from 2nd New Zealand Division, provoked into combat by Coke at the 8th Army leave centre in Bari, changed Coke's previously benign appearance for the worse. His nose, bent out of true by several degrees to its left, stayed in its new location and set there. This rearrangement brought consequential adjustments elsewhere. The right side of Coke's upper lip was pulled towards the bone and gristle it was fastened to. Coke, as simple and helpful as ever, now bore permanently an expression of sinister, leering callousness, like a mass murderer who does it for fun.

Coke was untroubled by this transformation. His mates were at first good-humouredly derisive and then became used to it. His officers showed initial aesthetic distaste but soon realized that, properly exploited, the new-look Coke was an asset. Prisoners taken in the confusion of a commando operation on a Dalmatian island or the Albanian coast soon became tractable when put in the care of Coke. Thoughts of escape, or reluctance to talk, withered fast at the sight of a sneering, trigger-happy sadist, cradling a Tommy gun in his arms, looking as if he was hoping for a false move that would provoke him to slaughter the lot.

Coke was equally effective with intransigent Balkan Communist political commissars. They thought twice before making ritual complaints about double-dealing capitalist allies, or the inadequacies of the Western fighting contribution compared with that of the Russian, when Coke was brought into play, strolling goonishly by in his faded green beret and his leather jerkin, a mindless, grinning psychopath drooling for blood.

Shortly after the German surrender in Italy in May 1945, No. 2 Commando Brigade returned by sea to Britain. They were to go on leave prior to going out to reinforce No. 3 Brigade in the Far East, where the war against Japan still continued. Coke sought an interview with the unit medical officer.

Coke explained that although he himself was unconcerned by his facial expression, his girlfriend might not be. He had not

102

seen her for two years and he wouldn't want to cause her distress. Was there any way in which the doctor could straighten out his nose and put his lip back in the right place?

The doctor was very fond of Coke. Coke had carried in wounded on his back to the regimental aid post during the Brac battle. Coke, himself shot in the shoulder, had refused to be sent back at Commachio and had worked away, whistling, helping the medical orderlies with the other wounded. Coke had done countless unobtrusive little kindnesses for the sick and wounded in Yugoslavia and Italy.

The doctor examined Coke's bent nose. To bend it back satisfactorily would require delicate surgery and the use of sophisticated instruments not carried on the inventory of a mobile aid post. The doctor told Coke that he could promise nothing but he would think it over. He would send for Coke if his thoughts led to something fruitful.

Three days later a distinguished London surgeon, responding to a request from an old pupil whom he respected, on behalf of a soldier who had more than earned his pay, performed without fee an operation for which his usual run of patients would have been skinned up to their bank manager's eyeballs.

A proud and grateful Coke, swathed in dressings, brought the surgeon's notes to the unit doctor. The doctor studied the notes and told Coke that the unveiling ceremony would be in ten days' time.

The nose, when finally let loose in the fresh air, was a masterpiece. Coke was widely congratulated and warned jocularly that the new version was so much of an improvement on the original, let alone the interim model, that his judy on Tyneside wouldn't recognize him.

Coke went out that night to celebrate. The largest man present in the bar of a Sussex pub was a Canadian lumberjack from a forestry company.

'No, I bloody won't,' said the doctor to Coke on the following morning, 'but at least you can tell her that it's bent round the other way now.'

103

NATURAL SELECTION

THE introduction in 1943 of psychiatrists to help assess the potential of officer candidates appearing before War Office selection boards was a measure that was not universally welcomed throughout the army. Some experienced commanding officers felt slighted. Their recommendations, based on years of professional judgement of the human capacity for leadership, were now to be subject to review in the light of what seemed to them to be a weird and imprecise pseudo-science.

The situation was made worse by the personal appearance of the people who practised this witch-doctory. With a few praiseworthy exceptions, so the critics considered, they were either scruffy and malformed or looked as if they were raving mad.

These entrenched attitudes stimulated a certain defensive diffidence among some of the psychiatrists.

The proposal put by one of them to a colonel in the Royal Army Service Corps at Catterick was thus advanced in a spirit of pessimistic shyness.

The colonel ran a training establishment. One of the courses for which he was responsible was for motor transport officers. Fifteen junior officers at a time came for instruction for a three-week period. Could the psychiatrist use these students for a research project designed to crosscheck the validity of the techniques in vogue at the selection boards?

The colonel asked suspiciously what this would involve. There was a crowded syllabus and he was damned if he would allow any distractions that would upset the students' concentration.

The psychiatrist said that there would be no disturbance of concentration at all. What he wanted to do was to make notes on the personality characteristics of recently commissioned officers to see if the right type of young leader was being picked. He could achieve this end by sitting unobtrusively at the back of lectures and so on, and simply observing behaviour patterns. His only call on their time would be to ask them to complete a questionnaire, which would take them about threequarters of an hour and which they could do when off duty.

The colonel said that the observation part of this suggested programme was out. If the students found themselves being peered at for hours on end by a silent quack, they would find it unsettling. What about this questionnaire? What were the questions?

The psychiatrist said that its general thrust was aimed at establishing whether these officers were suitably highly motivated and had reasonably well-integrated personalities capable of optimum performance in stressful situations. The colonel, who wouldn't have put it quite like that himself, said that that was all very well, but could he have some details?

The usual things, said the psychiatrist: an intelligence test, a short general knowledge quiz, some simple questions about personal ambitions, sexual experience and aspirations. The question that he himself had always found to give the most significant results was about being marooned on a desert island. If you were given the choice of one companion, which other student would you pick? From the answers to this, it became clear who the students themselves judged to be the man among them best endowed with resourcefulness, courage, reliability, endurance, cheerfulness in adversity and other qualities of leadership.

It was fascinating how individual estimates varied. He had tried it regularly on twenty-strong groups of selection board candidates. So far, no one candidate had been chosen by more than eight of his colleagues.

The colonel was less interested in desert islands than he was in an earlier class of inquiry. If all that prurient business about sex and ambition was left lying about on bits of paper, he said, there was a danger that it might fall into the wrong hands. Suppose the troops got hold of it? How could they be expected to respect an officer whom they knew to be, for example, a self-confessed foot fetishist who wanted to be a politician?

Confidentiality, said the psychiatrist, nettled, was central to the ethics of the medical profession. His records were kept under lock and key but in this instance, if the colonel was worried, he would happily take the protection of names a stage further than was usual. The purpose of the research was not to evaluate individuals. They had already been evaluated. What he wanted was an overall impression of whether current selection procedures were producing the right sort of people. Names were irrelevant. So far as he was concerned they could call themselves A, B and C, and so on, on the questionnaires.

There was just one thing though. It didn't happen very often, but it was not unknown for this kind of testing to expose a character flaw of such seriousness that immediate remedial or precautionary action was essential. He would look pretty silly if he identified a psychopath, or a coward, or a potential traitor, and could then describe him only as a subaltern known as G. Why didn't the colonel keep the master list, and allocate personally the As, Bs and Cs. It could be destroyed once the questionnaires had been analysed.

The colonel thought it over briefly and said okay. He had no faith in any of this mumbo-jumbo, but a recent Army Council instruction had been threateningly explicit about the need for improved cooperation by commanding officers with what the colonel had been told were known in the United States as shrinks.

The shrink departed. The colonel sent for a copy of the motor transport course nominal roll, wrote at random one of the letters from A to O against each name, and dictated to the orderly room clerk a one line letter, marked confidential. Fifteen stencilled duplicates were made, each was addressed individually, and they were distributed by the chief instructor to each student on the course.

The letters simply told the students that for the purposes of a forthcoming questionnaire which they would be asked to complete, they were to describe themselves by the letter of the alphabet that had been chosen for them.

The colonel then put the master list in his safe with a copy of the letter and forgot about them.

Two weeks later the shrink, looking unusually animated, asked to see him. He bore news.

'I've finished checking those questionnaires,' he said. 'There are some rather extraordinary findings about J.'

'What is he?' asked the colonel. 'A transvestite German spy?'

'Far from it. An exceptionally promising young officer. That's why I came to see you. I thought you might like to recommend that his CO should keep a special eye on him. He's got the makings of a real goer.'

'Oh yes?' said the colonel. He had no intention of being bounced into precipitate enthusiasm.

'It all came out in that desert island test I was telling you about. The maximum score we've ever had before is eight out of twenty. This chap J got 100 per cent. Every one of the other students chose him as a companion.'

The colonel opened his safe, took out the master list, poked about with his finger until he found J, and looked up.

'Runs a transport pool for top Allied brass in London,' he said. 'Name of Alice. I must say I wouldn't mind a stretch on a desert island with her myself.'

CHOOSE YOUR WEAPONS

For some months in 1944 the senior British officer on the Dalmatian island of Vis was Lieutenant Colonel Jack Churchill of the Manchester Regiment and No. 2 Commando.

Colonel Churchill was a versatile and unorthodox commander, with a private interest in items of weaponry regarded by some as having been superseded by the Industrial Revolution. He found it helpful, for example, when going into action to supplement his armoury with a claymore. Bagpipes, although strictly not weapons, also added an unusual garnishing to his personal kit list for battle.

There was more than a quirky nostalgia for militaria in his enthusiasm for these artifacts. He put them to practical use. A dozen or so Germans, confronted individually and in succession by an intimidating figure pointing a claymore at them, surrendered at Salerno without comment. The playing of 'Will ye no' come back again' on his pipes once indicated his wishes to a unit otherwise out of contact because Colonel Churchill's wireless had been destroyed by mortar fire.

He was also credited with an innovatory definition of the functions of a unit second in command: 'The job of the second in command is to hang around waiting for the colonel to get bumped off.'

One of the problems that he shared on Vis with his partisan opposite number was that German aircraft from the Yugoslav mainland came frequently to bomb the island from a low level. Colonel Churchill asked that light anti-aircraft guns be sent from Italy. Four Bofors and their Royal Artillery crews duly arrived, commanded by a captain.

Colonel Churchill greeted the captain warmly and told him without delay that after making a detailed study of the nature and pattern of the air attacks so far delivered he had decided exactly where each Bofors gun should be sited. They were to be put at points A, B, C and D, as marked on this map which the captain should take with him.

The gunner captain said that, with respect, the colonel seemed rather to be going about the matter in the wrong way. Anti-aircraft gunnery, like all gunnery, was a highly technical business. It was not for the colonel to start picking gunsites. If the colonel would define precisely the task for which the guns were required, i.e. to provide cover for Komiza harbour or whatever it was, he, the gunnery specialist, would select the positions from which his guns could best fulfil that task.

Colonel Churchill said that there was no need to bother about all that. He'd given a lot of thought to the thing. All the gunner had to do was to get moving and put his guns at A, B, C and D as already described.

The gunner said that, with renewed respect, it was essential that he do his job in his own way and in accordance with accepted practice common throughout the army. If the colonel would. . . .

Colonel Churchill said that he was losing patience with all this chatter. The guns were to be set up at points A, B, C and D, and that was all there was to it.

The gunner said, 'Very well, sir.' He had been given a direct order and he would obey it. He must, however, register a formal protest. He would like to make clear his view that if the detailed performance of his job was to be subject to outside interference by unqualified laymen, he might as well be armed with bows and arrows.

Colonel Churchill showed pleased surprise. He went to a cupboard and took out a bow and a quiverful of arrows. 'Are you interested in bows and arrows?' he asked eagerly.

109

SENSE OF TOUCH

On a dark, freezing cold winter's morning the officers of a wartime battalion of a Highland regiment plodded morosely through a bleak hutted camp to be addressed by their new brigade commander. There were several reasons why they were not looking forward to this encounter.

They didn't want a new brigadier, particularly not one like this man was said to be. They had liked and admired the previous incumbent, a brave and understanding leader, much decorated from the previous war. The story behind his departure had not, of course, been mentioned by him to them, but they knew that he had been sidetracked to a dead-end administrative job because he had stood up inflexibly for what they saw as their rights during a massive row with divisional headquarters.

They had dined him out on the previous night. It had been a sentimental and progressively noisy affair that had continued until the early hours.

On this chill morning few of them felt all that well. They mourned their departed boss. They resented the new man's refusal of an invitation to the dinner. They regarded his selection of 8 a.m. on the day after the dining out night for his introductory talk as a sinister foreshadowing of incivilities to come. They mistrusted his reputation as an ambitious and uninhibited new broom. They objected to his Lowland regimental background.

They filed silently into a large Nissen hut used normally for boxing competitions and weekend cinema shows. They sat in discontent, stood rigidly to attention when the brigadier was conducted in and introduced by their colonel, and sat down again when told that they might do so. They stared critically at the new management. It looked even worse than they had feared.

He was a trim, springy little man, with an unpleasantly healthy complexion. The gleamingly clear whites of his eyes were an affront to an audience that had been depleting the mess liquor stocks until four o'clock in the morning. His voice rasped. He expressed himself incisively and without tact.

His original intention, he said, had been to give them a brief rundown on his personal tactical doctrine, to be followed by an exposition of what he expected from each of them first in training, later in action. A quick look around the room had caused him to change his mind. He was no prude, but it was obvious to anyone with half an eye that for the majority of them the previous night had been one of gross overindulgence.

He would accordingly defer his talk on tactics to a date when they were in a better condition to absorb its lessons. He would now talk to them instead about physical fitness.

He did. They were appalled. It was a matter of personal and corporate pride to them, enshrined in long tradition, that, regardless of the extent of their off-duty libations, they were always alert and fit for work on the following morning. Their daily round was one of hard exercise. Now this sanctimonious little creep was complaining about their state of fitness without first testing it, and was giving out *Boy's Own* type helpful hints on the benefits that would flow from early nights, moderation in all things, and cold baths.

They gazed stolidly ahead. Captain Murdoch of D Company, a small man sitting behind two large ones, could take it no longer. He unfastened the map pocket on the left thigh of his battledress trousers, leaned forward until he was hidden from his brigadier's view, and withdrew a flat, silver hip flask. He partially restored the balance of his metabolism.

This was a mistake. Murdoch began to take an irrationally keen interest in all this suspect chat about clean living.

The brigadier changed gear from generalized exhortation

111

to grisly personal reminiscence offered as an example that his hearers might usefully follow. He described in detail his own early-morning routine. The instant wakefulness when his batman brought his tea. The leap from his bed, followed by press-ups. The first shock of icy bathwater, the invigorating splashing, the satisfying glow from his body as he towelled himself.

'At this point,' he said, 'the day really begins. I'm ready for anything. I feel rosy all over.'

Murdoch was upset. 'The poor, poor girl. Poor bloody Rosie,' he cried, prior to being placed under close arrest.

SMOKE SIGNAL

A free thing in life not rated among the best was the weekly issue, without charge, of a ration of V cigarettes to troops in the Middle East.

Speculation about the materials used in the construction of these smokes provided a constant topic of conversation. The chief component was agreed to be dried camel droppings, but there was interested discussion about what these were mixed with.

For some weeks Lance Corporal Carmichael of the Gordon Highlanders paid no attention to the provenance of V cigarettes, or indeed to much else. He was a patient in a surgical ward of a British General Hospital in Alexandria. For the first part of his stay he had been unconscious. A German 81-millimetre mortar bomb which burst within two yards of him had wounded him elaborately at Alamein.

He slowly pulled round. Piece by piece his manifold dressings diminished in size, began to be dispensed with altogether.

One stayed longer than the rest, a bandage around his eyes. He was not blinded, but both retinas had been affected. He was told that he must wait patiently in darkness until nature cured him. To ensure that his ultimate recovery of vision should not be put at risk by his doing something silly like pulling at his bandage in a moment of absent-mindedness or exasperation, he was kept in mild sedation. He dozed the days away.

He was in a light sleep one day when the ward sister brought company to his bedside. They were three young

113

British women, daughters of an embassy official and of a Cairo businessman. They had volunteered their services as nursing auxiliaries in the VAD. The sister had been charged with their elementary instruction. She had picked Carmichael as a demonstration model of the human body, fully furnished with all mechanisms in good functioning order. His additional qualification for the role was that since he was almost permanently asleep he was unlikely to complain.

The sister pointed to bits of Carmichael and named them. The girls took notes.

The lesson progressed to more practical matters, starting with the taking of a patient's temperature. Were any of the girls knowledgeable in that? One said yes. She knew medicine was different, but she'd done a year as a veterinary student at Edinburgh.

She was invited to demonstrate her skill. The sleeping Carmichael was bundled over onto his face. His pyjama trousers were pulled down roughly. She thrust the thermometer into his rectum.

The sister remarked that Carmichael was not a horse. There *were* times when rectal temperature readings of human patients were advisable, but the normal practice was to put the thermometer into the patient's mouth.

The former veterinary student had quick reflexes. In one fluid move she withdrew the thermometer, whipped Carmichael on to his back, and put the thermometer into his mouth.

All this activity brought Carmichael drowsily awake. He moved his lips and his tongue tentatively.

'First cigarette for six weeks,' he muttered bitterly, 'and it has to be a V.'

SWEAT AND DRUMS

To break into the bandroom in the middle of the night and set about the instruments with a pickaxe may seem at first glance to be a crime that raises questions about motive.

Who would do a thing like that, and why?

An extremist music critic? A pacifist opponent of military marches? A gambling syndicate taking no chances on the likelihood of having to pay out more than was tolerable after accepting too many bets at high odds on the number of times 'The Happy Wanderer' would be played in public during a specified calendar month?

The provost sergeant was untroubled by any of this psychological Hercule Poirot stuff. Alerted by a tip-off from informers whose attentions had been attracted by the sheer noise of the operation, he had, as he put it when the case came up for hearing, proceeded without delay to the bandroom and caught the accused red-handed. The accused had by then discarded his pickaxe and was standing in the middle of the wreckage holding the big drummer's leopardskin by its ears. He was trying to kick its teeth out.

The accused was the big drummer himself. The provost sergeant had formed the opinion that he had a grievance.

Asked if this was so, the big drummer said yes, he certainly had. It was to do with the heat. He had always taken a pride in his work and could say without boasting that when it came to big drumming he had few serious rivals. Those present with good memories would recall that photo of him in the

115

'NOR HAVE THE BLANKSHIRES EVER BROKEN RANKS OR RETREATED!'

programme for the Royal Tournament. It had been widely reproduced in the press.

The real point was that he had no objection to having to dress up on ceremonial occasions in all that fancy uniform. He liked it. What had particularly attracted him to the job in the first place, apart from the opportunity to get paid for exercising his drumming talents, was, in fact, the outfit. He had had a special affection for the leopardskin apron that hung almost to his knees in front and had the head slung over his shoulder. It had a remarkable effect on women.

That had been in the UK of course, where temperatures had been kept reasonable. Things were different in the Far

116

East. The band now wore lightweight drill uniforms when performing but, because of the nature of his speciality, he had been singled out for differential treatment. He had to wear his leopardskin over his drill tunic. In consequence he lost about half a stone in weight every time the band got down to work.

On reflection he was sorry for what he had done but he had had a few drinks beforehand and emotion had overtaken him.

The provost sergeant, asked if the accused when apprehended had said anything to suggest that he felt remorse about the gravity of the offence, misunderstood the question. He said, 'Yessir,' and thumbed open his notebook. 'His exact words were,' said the provost sergeant, ' "You've bothered me all me life you bastard." I think he was addressing the leopard.'

After sentence had been passed, arrangements were made with a local taxidermist to keep the leopardskin in store until the battalion moved to the United Kingdom or anywhere else with a temperate climate.

THE MUSIC OF MARS

A rich, untapped vein of material lies available to anyone wishing to study the correlation in recent major wars between national military attitudes and the martial music that once inspired those members of a country's armed forces who were not tone deaf. At first glance it seems fairly easy to isolate trends that transcended frontiers. There is, for example, a recognizable distinction in several countries between the official and the unofficial. The French became ceremonially emotional about *la Gloire* and *la Patrie* but on the march sang about women with names like Madelon and various Cochin-Chinese ladies. The Germans oscillated between thunderous declarations of intent to march against England, supplemented by lachrymose commemorative stuff about Horst Wessel, and the sweetest Second World War song of them all, 'Lilli Marlene'.

British practice differed only in degree from that of the French and Germans. The assistance of God was invoked confidently at government level, and firm opinions were put to music about the advisability of territorial expansion and the frustration of foreigners. The personal war aims of the troops were expressed more cynically. If their songs are to be taken at their face value, which they should not be, the major preoccupations of the British fighting man in both world wars were with nonstop sexual congress, getting and staying drunk, and wishing complicated retribution, mostly to do with accidents in lavatories, upon sergeant majors.

It would be a rash researcher who would try to draw firm deductions from these unrepresentative and superficial samples. The field is large and complex. Almost the whole of Europe, much of Asia, some of Africa, and all of North America took part in one or both of the two world wars. In which of these other armies, and in what manner, did day-to-day military choristry diverge from government-sponsored patriotism with musical accompaniment?

There are many related questions to be answered.

A quotation, the words of the march past of an Indian Army regiment of impeccable fighting credentials, illustrates in a small way how much work there is to be done on this subject:

> There's a boy across the river
> With a bottom like a peach.
> But alas! I cannot swim.

TRICK CYCLIST

Iɴ the manner exemplified by the great Duke of Marl-
borough who, on return from campaigning in Flanders,
pleased his Duchess three times before taking off his
boots (or so *she* said), Corporal Noakes of 7th Armoured
Division devoted his disembarkation leave to making up for
lost time.

The time, expressed in terms of Noakes's recreational pre-
ferences, had been lost in Egypt, Libya and Tunisia. The
cities had offered limited solace, heavily circumscribed by the
military police and the Royal Army Medical Corps, but
Noakes's normal habitat had been the desert. He had been
one of the original Desert Rats. For nearly three years he had
wandered up and down the desert, fighting insanitary Italians
and dangerous Germans. He had been variously jubilant,
disappointed, puzzled, cynical, happy, unhappy, too hot, too
cold and occasionally, although he had kept the symptoms
rigorously hidden, frightened out of his wits. A regular soldier,
he had found none of this surprising.

He had quite liked the desert, if rather less than he would
later claim had been the case. Its main drawback, as he saw it,
was the conspicuous absence of his favourite amenity.

After a debilitating disembarkation leave Noakes returned
to his armoured regiment. It was being re-equipped, rein-
forced and retrained for the Normandy campaign. Noakes's
squadron was billeted near a small country town. There were
busy days and nights of intensive training. Old sweats like
Noakes were invaluable during this period. They drew on
their experience, passed on useful hints to the reinforcements

120

and told some impressive lies, most of which were harmless. A few were socially beneficient.

The desert veterans were easily distinguishable from the newcomers by a self-confident maturity and a specialized and almost incomprehensible vocabulary concerned with wadis, gharries, bints, shuftis and similar exotica. Also, they wore the ribbon of the Africa star. This was the colour of sand and bore thin vertical stripes, dark blue, scarlet and light blue, to represent each of the three services. There was a figure 8 in the middle of the ribbon to show that they had served in the 8th Army.

Noakes, in this new environment, early made the acquaintance of two ladies, mother and daughter. Friendship ripened rapidly. There were a number of administrative obstacles to the process, brought about largely by the erratic hours and unpredictable commitments of a soldier rehearsing for a large-scale operation. Noakes showed resilience. The ladies were adaptable. The obstacles were circumvented.

Like everyone else preparing for Normandy, Noakes received a heavy indoctrination about the need for security. He was repeatedly lectured, exhorted and threatened. He thought the requirement sensible and found its implementation unexacting. He was tight-lipped to the ladies about his military activities, saying only, when necessary, that he would be 'busy'.

Indeed he actually improved upon the security briefings he had been given. He declined to tell the ladies his surname, arguing that any information, however trivial seemingly, could be of use to enemy intelligence operatives trying to compile the Allied order of battle. Using a phrase that he borrowed from one of the then popular movie magazines, he told them not to call him. He would call them.

In circumstances duplicated in towns and villages all over the south and west of England at the time, Noakes's regiment was found one morning to have vanished. It had stolen away with necessary circumspection to its sealed-off, pre-invasion concentration area. A permanent administrative headquarters, commanded by an elderly dug-out full colonel, was given

the task of tying up the loose ends left by all departing sol-
diery. The colonel passed a busy few weeks dealing with
claims for flattened crops, structural damage caused by care-
lessly driven tanks, unresolved mysteries in public houses,
and the accidental incineration of a requisitioned vicarage
during an officers' mess guest night that got out of hand.

The colonel was also confronted by the two ladies. They
were, they said, interested in news of somebody known to
them only as Fred, to whom they were devoted. They
reminisced with uninhibited zeal about the arrangements that
they had made for Fred's comfort and welfare. They would
have done even better by him, they explained, had they not
been hampered by two limitations. The first arose from Fred's
irregular working hours. They had never known when he
would turn up or how long he would stay. The second problem was that the mother lived four miles from her daughter.
They had given much thought to how to mitigate these disabilities of time and space and had found a simple solution.
The mother had lent Fred her bicycle. Fred, in his off-duty
moments, would pedal to the mother, enjoy her hospitality,
pedal to the daughter, enjoy hers, and when time was up
would cycle away to continue in his preparation for the next
stage of the fight for his country.

Both mother and daughter were now pregnant. They would
very much like to get in touch with Fred.

The colonel suppressed some old-fashioned revulsion, had
confused thoughts about English roses, harpies and war aims,
and pressed for descriptive detail about Fred. Even though
Fred had clearly been a sensibly reticent operator, the hunt for
his identity could be narrowed by imaginative cross-
examination. Whoever he was, he must be the bearer of
recognizable military labels. Patient questioning confirmed
the colonel's view that the two women had the moral standards of rabbits. They also seemed to him to be half-witted.
But he slowly assembled a sort of identikit picture of a corporal who wore the divisional insignia of a Desert Rat of 7th
Armoured, wore a pretty little coloured ribbon with a figure 8
on it, and was a gifted linguist. This last seemed unlikely and

proved to be so. Fred apparently qualified because he referred to a ditch as a wadi.

The colonel studied his notes. He summed up for the ladies. He thanked them for the care with which they had answered his inquiries. He was not, he said, altogether sure how many corporals named Fred with desert experience were currently serving with 7th Armoured Division, but whatever the total it was, so to speak, manageable.

The corps of military police would be asked to set inquiries in train at once, but, as the ladies would doubtless have read in the press or heard on the wireless, the division was at present in action in Normandy and there might be some delay before the matter was resolved. They could, however, rest assured that the full force of the law would be invoked. If the corporal – er, Fred – contested the evidence, there might have to be a court hearing, but if they won the case they could expect maintenance payments for the child – er, children – and possibly compensation as well.

The ladies said that they wouldn't want any unpleasantness like that. They had come to ask if they could have their bicycle back.

FORGERY

WITH the exception of the United States Army, the rich uncle of the arena, the combatants in the Normandy campaign depended upon some fairly elderly devices to sustain many of their secondary activities.

Thus while German Panzer divisions with their superb Tiger and Panther tanks had a full complement of tracked and wheeled vehicles to carry their supporting infantry, German infantry formations relied heavily upon horsedrawn wagons for their administrative needs.

Allied pilots in ruinously expensive aeroplanes dominated the skies. The ships of the Royal Navy, the guns of the Royal Artillery, the tanks of the Royal Armoured Corps were contemporary triumphs of sophisticated industrial production. Farther away from the shop window lurked organisms furnished less lavishly.

One of these was a detachment of the Royal Electrical and Mechanical Engineers equipped with a mobile coke-fired forge. Some inspired improviser had calculated that this ponderous gadget, though unsuitable for use too close to where the real rough stuff was in progress, could offer a valuable supplement to the work of the field workshops that dealt in the repair of salvaged tanks, self-propelled guns and the like.

The primary role of the mobile forge team was seen as the straightening out of bits of abandoned, damaged vehicles with a view to their subsequent incorporation in new models assembled from disparate cannibalized parts.

The REME detachment went ashore on D+14 and immediately met with misfortune. The subaltern commanding it wandered off on some unauthorized tourism, strayed into an uncleared minefield, lost a foot on a *schu* mine, and was evacuated. His sergeant, always tense, was reduced to nervous collapse by this event. He was evacuated too. The detachment was left under the command of a corporal, an admirably qualified and practical technician, but out of his depth in the strange circumstances in which he now found himself. He neither knew where he was nor where he was supposed to go.

The naval beachmaster here intervened. He adopted, some would say confiscated, the mobile forge unit. He was a forceful and tidy-minded officer. The beach and its exits were littered with landing craft with bent ramps, brewed-up jeeps, trucks and a scout car, and miscellaneous pieces of unidentifiable metallic junk. There was plenty of scope for REME amidst all this. If somebody somewhere felt badly deprived by the absence of a coke-fired forge, he would sooner or later come looking for it. In the meantime there was useful work for it where it was.

The beachmaster told the corporal to start forging outside a wrecked house near one of the beach exits. The corporal did so with relief. Responsibility had been lifted from him. He had been given clear instructions. He was a willing and conscientious operator. The grounds of the wrecked house soon looked like an eccentrically run do it yourself automobile assembly plant. The sound of metal being bashed merged discreetly in the background uproar that echoed intermittently from the line.

The beachmaster was pleased with the activities of his hijacked forge and equally pleased that its rightful proprietor had after ten days made no effective attempt to recover it. There was, however, a difficulty that would soon have to be faced.

The forge unit, self-contained and with its own transport, had arrived with rations for two weeks and with four tons of coke. The two weeks were nearly up and the diligence of the corporal was such that a coke shortage was imminent. The beachmaster would have to indent for replenishments to be brought across the English Channel. They would be supplied without delay, but delivery would be followed by questions. Who were these unaccounted people on his ration strength? What conceivable use could he have for four tons of coke?

The beachmaster's counter to this potential threat to his forge came in two parts. Rations were easy. Unit strengths varied inconstantly with casualties and replacements. There were plenty of spare boxes of compo within the beachmaster's zone of influence. An adequate number went to the corporal.

Coke for the forge required more devious action. The beachmaster took his problem to his friend and neighbour, the American beachmaster, a highly efficient performer who operated in an ambience of genial prodigality, undisturbed by bureaucratic nit-picking.

Sure, said this praiseworthy ally, no sweat. Easily fixed. He'd signal the request on his evening list and an American LCM would be diverted to the British beach when the next lift came over.

It was in this manner that the REME detachment came into possession of four tons of Coca-Cola, deposited by an American landing craft crew who said that back home they usually measured the stuff different.

BILLET DOUX

IN the middle months of 1945 many civilians in the
United Kingdom were discommoded by what were
known to the Army as initiative tests. These were concentrated at this time because the war against the Germans
had been won, and the war against the Japanese had yet to be
so. Soldiers who had recently been fighting in Italy and in
northwest Europe, and who were due to go to the Far East,
would become stale and bloody-minded if subjected to too
much repetitive conventional training. Why not give them
something to alleviate boredom that at the same time would
foster useful qualities of self-reliance and opportunism? Give
them tasks of no direct military significance that would test
their resourcefulness and provide some entertainment.

Thus it was that actresses' dressing rooms in provincial
theatres were invaded by courteous soldiers asking for
souvenir pieces of underwear, to be accompanied by autographed assurances of goodwill. Headmasters of boarding
schools, selected by recently left subalterns who felt that the
more trouble the old bastard was put to the better, were asked
by persuasive junior NCOs to put their signatures to meaningless petitions about dog dirt control in neighbouring towns.

Private Wright, who was based at Bexhill in Sussex, was
told to make his way under his own steam to the north of
England and to parade outside the Liver building in Liverpool along with the rest of his section, three days after they left
Bexhill. The rules of this particular game, enforced by a
rigorous inspection before departure, were that no man
should start with more than two shillings in his pocket. Theft

or violence would lead to severe disciplinary sanctions and possibly civil or criminal prosecution.

The obvious way to go, chosen by most, was to hitchhike. The few civilian drivers with petrol rations were sympathetic to travelling servicemen. Army and RAF trucks tended to travel farther than private motorists, and were similarly helpful. Wright hitchhiked to London and felt a sudden urge to get the rest of the thing done in one uninterrupted move. He walked to Euston Station.

He had no difficulty in boarding a train. He waited until a minute before its departure and then bustled past the platform ticket barrier amidst a welter of last-moment travellers hurrying for the carriage doors. His next opponent would be the train's ticket collector, on his mobile check of passengers' paid-up status.

Wright was unworried. He'd face that problem when it came to him. At its worst, he could jump out when the train slowed, or for that matter let himself be put off by officialdom at an intermediate stop. In either case he would have knocked a sizeable leg off his journey. It would not be the uninterrupted ride he hoped for, but a not bad second best.

The only other people in his compartment were two sailors of the Royal Navy. He soon realized, listening to them talk, that when it came to cheap lifts on railways he was an amateur, fleaweight class. The two matelots had a system.

It wasn't a system for *free* travel, they explained to Wright. It merely cut the cost by half. They had one ticket between them. The man without the ticket had, like Wright, boarded by crashing the barrier in the last-minute rush. Long and successful practice had taught them the likely time of the ticket inspector's tour of the compartments. Before his arrival, the two would withdraw to the lavatory and lock themselves in.

The ticket inspector would knock on the door. One sailor would say, 'Sorry, can't move,' and would push the ticket through the gap at the bottom of the door. The inspector would punch holes in it and pass it back. Wait three minutes for luck, and out and away. Dead simple.

The inspector, they said, would by now be about starting on his rounds. Time they left for the lavatory. They went.

Wright gave them a two-minute start, walked along the corridor, and hammered on the lavatory door.

'Ticket inspector,' he called.

A voice said, 'Sorry, can't move.' A return ticket to Liverpool was thrust under the door.

Wright put it into his pocket and made his way to a compartment at the far end of the train.

POSITIVE VETTING

ADMIRERS of improvisation in the field of veterinary technique will wish to unite in respect for the unnamed farrier sergeant of the Royal Horse Artillery who at Umballa in 1898 used a fire-engine to give an enema to an elephant.

'I WANT THREE VOLUNTEERS'

SINK OF INIQUITY

DURING the closing stages of the fight at Arnhem, when 1st Airborne Division was being inexorably squeezed in upon itself by German armour, self-propelled guns, and every other weapon that could be brought to bear upon the perimeter, one of the division's padres went on his customary rounds as a bearer of spiritual and physical consolation.

It was a dangerous form of parish visiting. The relieving 2nd Army was held up. Most resupply drops had either gone astray or had been postponed because of bad weather. The airborne soldiers, armed only with what they had carried on their persons from the dropping zone of several days earlier, were taking on elements of two Panzer divisions and supporting troops, all backed by a generous provision of ammunition and reinforcements delivered on wheels.

The padre picked his way carefully through ruined suburban gardens and crumbled houses. He paused at intervals, lying flat on his stomach as showers of whining mortar bombs crashed noisily nearby. He sprinted over patches of open ground covered by spandaus. He arrived, through the back door, at a badly knocked about small house, one of a terrace.

From the front of the house came a series of thunderous bangs, followed by three bursts of Bren and some terse bad language. The padre went towards what had been the sitting room and entered cautiously. His caution was a product of good manners, not self-preservation. He was a transient visitor. The people he was calling on lived here. Any unnecessary attention the padre attracted would be to their detriment, not his.

Two dirty, red-eyed, unshaven soldiers in stained parachute smocks lay in the wrecked sitting room. They themselves had knocked the glass from the windows but the rest of the damage was from external causes. They were behind a barricade of mattresses and what looked like the contents of the house's airing cupboard, set up loosely on the side of the room away from the window. The ceiling sagged. The walls were pitted, and a coating of flaked plaster lay over a jumble of splintered furniture.

The padre, as grimed, stubbled and tired as the soldiers, eased up beside them. He put on his best pastoral smile and asked how things were going.

They explained that they had passed the morning having a bit of a ding-dong with German infantry in the houses on the other side of the street. They were more or less on top in the shooting contest between the windows, but a mortar had now been brought into play from behind the German house. At least two 88s also joined in from time to time.

It had been a lively few hours. The Germans had thrown everything at them except the kitchen sink.

At this early point in the discussion there came a resurgence of fluttering shrieking sounds, followed by some deafening explosions overhead. The sagging ceiling gave way in a landslide of shattered beams and plaster. Something heavy fell through the hole with a crash. When the flakes and dust had cleared, and all three had said 'Yes' to the others' 'You okay?', the thing that had come through the ceiling was seen to be a kitchen sink.

'I know the bastards are close,' said one of the Parachute Regiment soldiers dourly, 'but I hadn't realized they could hear what we were saying.'

ECONOMIC REGULATOR

Two days after the German surrender in Italy in May 1945, a bombardier and a gunner from a field regiment of the Royal Artillery, driving in a scout car, were approached by a sedentary-looking German officer. The German, who spoke no English, was only too glad to give himself up. He indicated by mime that the Italian partisans would cut his throat if he didn't.

He led the bombardier to a group of vehicles parked in concealment in a vineyard. Before being taken away, he handed over a bunch of keys. The bombardier used the keys, examined the trucks, and found that his captive had been a field paymaster. The weight of undistributed notes lodged in four safes in a vehicle equipped as an office suggested that recent operational pressures had left large numbers of the Wehrmacht badly in arrears.

The bombardier was an open-hearted man. Willing friends helped him to distribute his find throughout the battery. There was no finicking about with signatures or accounting. There was so much of the stuff that anyone who wanted any was simply advised to help himself to what he could conveniently carry.

It took little time for this infusion of capital to seep through the economy of the small town on the Lombardy plain where the battery was billeted. At a time of Italian national impoverishment the town began to flourish unnaturally. Street stalls selling farm produce, wine and ice cream to the soldiers at high prices proliferated. Two new blackmarket restaurants opened. A growing horde of scented female strangers

133

assembled. Domestic service became a growth industry. Wine-sipping, lounging gunners offered friendly advice to paid help on how to burnish cap badges and blanco webbing equipment.

Economists in the Allied military government started to pay attention to this curious local inflationary boom. They asked questions and sent a bilingual Intelligence Corps sergeant with glasses and a clipboard to do an informal cost-of-living survey.

The battery commander became concerned. That some money taken from German prisoners was in circulation had been evident for some time. Few gunners had bothered to draw their pay. The battery commander held pragmatic views on the ethics of looting. Stealing private property from civilian houses was disgusting, deserved heavy punishment, and got it. If cold, hungry soldiers supplemented their rations with occasional liberated chickens or eggs, that was okay, provided that they threatened no violence, didn't overdo it, and paid up if caught. If captured enemy troops were relieved of their small change before being sent to the rear, that was okay too. He had no sympathy for the plunderers of half Europe. Besides, if front-line troops didn't help themselves, less deserving rear-area guards would.

He had assumed that the current opulence of his command was a product of the take from the thousands of surrendered Germans that they had recently processed. He now recognized that he had been wrong. He made discreet inquiries through his battery captain and the battery sergeant major, stressing that he sought information, not retribution. It took little time to uncover the truth, roughly, about the German field paymaster.

The full battery was paraded and addressed by its leader. It was a casually elliptical oration, shot through with mixed metaphors about not biting off more than you could chew of the meat of the goose that laid the golden eggs, *et cetera*. It suggested a remedy for the local financial crisis. The remedy required popular cooperation, democratic organization and goodwill. The alternative would be an absolutely hellish dis-

134

ciplinary inquiry, mounted from outside the regiment, by legalistic pedants intent on locking up as many people as they could for as long as possible. The parade was dismissed, with instructions to think over alternative A.

Later in the morning, word was passed to the battery commander that the military equivalent of shop stewards had examined his proposals and had endorsed them as sound and equitable.

By lunchtime a narrow rectangular enclosure surrounded by canvas screens had been set up. Internally it was equipped not unlike an electoral polling station. Further screens shielded a long trestle table to which were bolted six metal PIAT ammunition boxes. The battery craftsmen had soldered the lids of these shut and had cut slits, large enough to take wads of banknotes but too small for the insertion of a human hand, in the tops of each. Another table, for the tellers, was placed at the entrance to the corral.

The afternoon parade was an informal affair confined to a rollcall and the forming of an orderly queue. The queue filed slowly towards the shielded boxes. Names were ticked off on the nominal rolls held by the tellers, selected by soviet. One at a time, each man moved to the privacy of the inner screen and put his surplus loot into a slit in an ammunition box.

When the last man had passed through, a blanket was spread on the tellers' table. The boxes were unbolted from the trestle table and prised open by the craftsmen, in the presence of witnesses from each subsection. The battery commander presided over the count, conducted by the tellers. The battery quartermaster sergeant sorted the notes by denomination into bundles and fastened them with elastic bands. The money was locked into boxes recovered from the captive paymaster's truck, taken to battery headquarters and placed under guard.

The battery commander reported to regimental headquarters that in the course of a general tidying up of his area, a previously undiscovered and well-camouflaged German field paymaster's abandoned vehicles had been found. He would have the money delivered under escort if someone would tell him where to deliver it.

RHQ replied that 8th Army headquarters would be pleased by this news. A German paymaster in a prisoner-of-war cage had recently been interrogated. He was none too bright, and couldn't read a map, but he had stated categorically that when he gave himself up he had left behind him, at a location that he was unable to identify, the lira equivalent of £120,000 sterling. The 8th Army and military government people had feared that it might have been found and abstracted by civilians or Communist partisans.

The battery commander, a conventional believer in the hierarchical ordering of military affairs, said, 'Oh Christ.' He reached his second unpalatable decision in two days. He would have to consult the shop stewards again. The sum contributed behind the canvas screens had been the lira equivalent of £138,000.

NO HOME, SWEET NO HOME

SERGEANT Peter O'Kelly of No. 4 Commando was seriously wounded by a mortar bomb in Normandy in July 1944. His recovery and convalescence were prolonged. By the time he was fit for duty the war in Europe had ended. By the time he reached Bombay on a troopship as a reinforcement for No. 3 Commando Brigade, which, when he left Britain, was ready in India for an assault landing in Malaya, the war against Japan had ended too.

O'Kelly was told in Bombay that 3 Brigade had gone to occupy Hong Kong. Shipping was overextended. His priority was low. He would have a long wait in a transit camp before he could move on to where he had to go.

O'Kelly disliked the transit camp. He also made a careful assessment of the personal position in which he now found himself. He had volunteered to fight in the war. The war was over. His moral obligations had ended with its conclusion. He had no particular wish to go to Hong Kong. He had less wish to stay in the transit camp. He wasn't in all that much of a hurry to go home either and, given the size of the waiting list for places on ships, would be unlikely to get there for a long time anyway. If he could choose, what would he really like?

Well, what he'd really like would be about six months comfortable relaxation in India, paid for by the Army and untainted by any tiresome requirement to do any work. O'Kelly requested an interview with the commanding officer of the transit camp, a major.

O'Kelly said that he wished to be RTUd.

The major said that unsatisfactory cadets in officer training

137

establishments could be returned to unit, but O'Kelly wasn't an officer cadet. O'Kelly, with the menacing courtesy he used on these occasions, said that he wasn't talking about officer cadets. He was talking about the Army Commandos, of whom he was one. All were volunteers. Part of the arrangement under which they served was that they could either be RTUd for inadequate performance or behaviour, or could themselves ask to be RTUd if they no longer fancied the life. He no longer fancied the life. What he was now putting forward was a formal request, as was his right, to be returned to a battalion of the infantry regiment from which he had volunteered for the Commandos.

The major said that this private army stuff was all news to him. Assuming it to be true, he had no status in the matter. If O'Kelly had some sort of funny contract with the Commandos, only the Commandos could release him from it.

O'Kelly put on a look of sinister sympathy and expressed understanding of the major's difficulty. Since the major was, so to speak, *in loco parentis*, he was presumably empowered to act as the agent of 3 Commando Brigade. If he had no such authority, why not get it? A signal to Hong Kong would do the trick.

The major, who had other things to attend to and who was beginning to find the continued presence of O'Kelly nervously unsettling, agreed. He pointed out, though, that the realignment of O'Kelly's role in the Army was not a subject for burning up the wires. He would send a written message. It would be of low priority and might even have to go by sea. The reply might take weeks.

This brought O'Kelly smoothly into the next part of his pitch. He assured the major that he was much more concerned with the principle of the thing than with its mechanics. Now that matters had been set in train, his mind was at rest. The initial move had, however, introduced a certain delicacy into the situation as the major would, of course, have recognized.

The major hadn't recognized it. He said so.

O'Kelly said that the point was that he was now in a sort of military limbo. He'd applied to be RTU'd. Until the application was approved, which according to the major could take weeks, O'Kelly belonged to nobody. He had cut his connection with the Commandos but had not been posted to his parent unit.

In this peculiar state of suspension it would be embarrassing, improper even, for him to continue in the transit camp. Think of the disciplinary complexities alone. If, for example, he put somebody on a charge, and the man disputed his authority to give a lawful order, what was the answer? Was O'Kelly a sergeant, or was he not? He had certainly been one in the Commandos, which he had now left, but he had held no stripes in the regiment he had yet to rejoin.

Discipline was only one problem. Could he continue to use the sergeants' mess? Was he eligible to be orderly sergeant? Possibilities for confusion were endless. It seemed to him that it would be fairest to everyone, not least the major, if he, O'Kelly, were to be kept on the strength of the transit camp for pay purposes only and otherwise be ordered to keep discreetly out of the way.

If the major was worried about his food and accommodation, he could rest easy. There were friends from his racing days in Ireland living not far away.

Prolonged formal leave was, of course, out of the question, but a condoned displacement would. . . .

The major, who had been contemplating gloomily the prospect of repetitive interviews with a balefully smiling O'Kelly daily conjuring up fresh legalistic angles about his Commando privileges, felt relief at this suggested solution. The one characteristic he had in common with the fellow was a shared view of the undesirability of having him in his transit camp.

O'Kelly enjoyed the next few weeks. His racing friends introduced him to others. Since nobody knew what he was, and he didn't bother to explain, he moved comfortably among clubs and cocktail parties, rode horses, did some shooting and played golf. He travelled widely, financed by the pay that had accumulated during his long spell in hospital, and which he transferred to rupees by means that would have agitated the exchange control authorities.

He had almost forgotten that he was still in the Army when he was summoned back to the transit camp. His application to be returned to unit, he was told personally by the major, had been approved.

'Your orders are to leave for the nearest battalion of your regiment as soon as possible. The Movements people will find out where it is, and arrange transport. What *is* your regiment, by the way?' added the major, feeling affable at a problem solved.

'Irish Guards, sir.'

'Oh Christ,' said the major.

'Yes,' said O'Kelly.

The Brigade of Guards did not serve east of Suez.

He collected the backpay that had built up for him at the transit camp and went off for several more months of his idyll, no longer claimed by one organization, unclaimable by another. His turn for a place in a troopship came up at the right moment. He disembarked in time for instant demobilization.

Eighteen months later, an informal meeting of the ex-Service Association of Trinity College, Dublin, met to draft representations to the British Ministry of Education on the need to increase ex-servicemen's grants. Facts were needed. A quick check around the table confirmed that, with one exception, everybody present was being paid £180 per year.

The exception was Peter O'Kelly. His grant was £210. Asked how he had persuaded the Ministry to show this unique generosity, the manipulator of Commando Group, the Brigade of Guards, and the commanding officer of an Indian transit camp was less than expansive.

'You haven't a horse to keep,' he explained enigmatically.

NINE GREEN BATTLES

IT was widely conceded by those who soldiered alongside them that the 2nd New Zealand Division was one of the finest fighting formations on the Allied side during the Second World War. They had proved it repeatedly in Greece, Crete, the Western Desert and Italy. The main dissentients from this assessment were 2NZ Div. themselves. They would delete 'one of'.

When, at the close of hostilities, the survivors went home, they took part good-humouredly in Victory parades, national, regional and local. These ceremonies were reported upon in detail in the newspapers. A slightly embarrassed young lieutenant colonel, anxious to return to rational life on his sheep farm, but willing to give the public a treat, led one of these parades in a rural town. The coverage given by the local paper was elaborate. The event was described in detail. Extensive background pieces were furnished on the more memorable achievements of individual returned warriors. The exploits which had won the young colonel the DSO and the MC were recalled in full. His manifold wounds were analysed. Nothing could be more fitting, the write-up ended, than that the local representatives of 2NZ Div., worthy heirs of the incomparable 1NZ Div. of the First World War, should be led on this triumphal occasion by this bottle-scarred veteran.

The colonel, a relatively temperate man, telephoned the editor to propose a correction to this slur on his off-duty habits. The editor was contrite and cooperative. Full amends would be made in the next edition.

'DORIS SENDS HER LOVE AND HAS ASKED ME TO PLAY "DEEP IN THE HEART
OF TEXAS" AS A REMINDER OF THEM ALL AT SHEPHERD'S BUSH'

The apology was thorough. The colonel's deeds of valour
and his surgical history were aired once more. The inadequate
performance of the compositor was touched on scathingly.
The whole unfortunate incident was wrapped up in an inci-
sive editorial last paragraph.

Let there be no misunderstanding about this lapse, for which we
take full responsibility. We did not, repeat not (as they say in the
Army), mean to print that this local son was bottle-scarred. As will
have been evident to all our readers, the description should have
been that he was battle-scared.

FATTED CALF AT THE GATE

THE neutrality of the Irish Free State in the Second World War generated some unusual consequences. One of them was that one tenth of the Irish Regular Army deserted and joined the British armed forces.

Among these temporarily displaced transferrers of allegiance was a man named Vincent Cullen. His father was a farmer in a small way in County Mayo. Mr Cullen senior, a widower, had in his time fought for the British in the Connaught Rangers at Gallipoli and in Serbia. He had subsequently fought against the British in Ireland in 1920 in the Irish Republican Army, an organization whose survivors are not enamoured of successors who have adopted the same name.

Mr Cullen senior was a famously taciturn man, of invincible inconsistency. His son, who after all had simply reversed his father's sequence of profession, was, he confided to his few intimates, a source of worry to him. The fellow lacked dedication. Kept darting around from one thing to another. With an outlook like that, he had all the makings of a sure-fired, guaranteed failure.

Vincent Cullen saw the war through with the Irish Brigade of 78 Division. The brigade embraced battalions of the Inniskilling Fusiliers, the Royal Irish Fusiliers and the London Irish Rifles. They fought in Tunisia, Sicily, and all the way up Italy. Between actions, its Northern Irish Protestant commander took time off to lead a representative delegation of the Catholic faithful and the Protestant curious to pay a formal call upon the Pope, after which the pipes and drums beat

143

retreat in the Vatican. Young Irish seminarians roared delighted applause as the band, supervised by a Presbyterian drum major ('Not to worry, sir, we'll give wee Popie a blow'), worked their way rousingly through 'The Boys of Wexford', 'The Wearing of the Green', and similar patriotic renderings. On other occasions it was not unknown for the Irish tricolour to be flown at brigade headquarters. It was a spiritedly nostalgic, ecumenical, tolerant formation, its eccentricities disregarded because of its effectiveness.

In this ambience Vincent Cullen felt entirely at home. By 1945 he was a sergeant, twice wounded and once decorated. He volunteered to stay on in the postwar army. He was accepted without question. Experienced senior NCOs of proved resourcefulness and reliability were people to be cherished.

During the late 1940s and early 1950s Cullen served in Egypt, Palestine and Malaya. Egypt, aside from a riot or two, was peaceful. The Hagganah and the Stern Gang made Palestine less so. Chinese Communist terrorists in Malaya added to the variety of Cullen's operational experience.

In ten years Cullen had not been back to Ireland. He was unable to take leave there prior to his departure for Tunisia in 1942 because as an Irish Army deserter he would have risked arrest. Later, after the war was over and the Irish government had amnestied all deserters, he was either abroad or, whilst briefly in Britain, preoccupied with impermanent love.

He decided upon a visit home in 1952 after continuously crowded, and at times downright dangerous, service. He felt misgivings. There had been a desultory exchange of dutiful letters between father and son during his journeyings, but from the paternal end these had shown some absence of warmth. This chilliness could be partly discounted by the consideration of the proposition that a man economical of the spoken work was unlikely to be extravagant with the written. None the less, a skein of recognizably subdued disapproval was evident in the correspondence. There was a notable reluctance to commiserate over setbacks or to applaud modest achievement. When you wrote that you were in hospital

144

recovering from wounds to both legs, don't worry, it'll be okay, and, by the way, they've given me the Military Medal, it would have been nice to get in response something more enheartening than that two cows were in calf and the weather was holding up well. Cullen senior seemed to be no easier to placate than he ever had been.

Vincent Cullen thus began his homecoming with apprehension. He had been shot at, and hit twice, by Germans, Italians, Arabs, Jews and Malayan Chinese. He had faced recurrences of these pieces of hostility with a wary indifference. He found, surprisingly and disturbingly, that a background of sustained physical courage was of no help in a confrontation with his formidable father. The nearer he approached home, the more he felt like a nervous small boy.

It was a slow, complicated journey. Cullen, bulging muscularly through a civilian blue suit, hair cut short at back and sides, shoes glistening like high-grade anthracite, travelled by B. & I. boat from Liverpool to the North Wall in Dublin. A slow train and two consecutive country buses carried him westward. The second left him outside a crossroads pub, low and whitewashed, and with a green-painted corrugated iron roof.

The tangy, evocative smell of turf smoke, drifting from the pub's chimney, hung in the air. There were low hills and small fields and stone walls, and waving white bog cotton behind long stacks of cut turf. Inconstant clouds scudded in from the Atlantic, masking the spring evening sun intermittently, changing the texture of the light, adjusting enchantingly the intensity of the browns and mauves and greens. Cullen felt sudden, overpowering emotion. This was his own place. He was home. An indication, just a small one, from his father of affection and understanding would complete this altogether unexpected sensation of sentimental euphoria.

Too much to hope for? He would see. He had always been an optimist. He hefted the two heavy suitcases and the grips with the presents for his father. There was a pebble from the Garden of Gethsemane, and a leather wallet from Port Said, and a set of *mengkuang* table mats from Malaya. He stepped out strongly for the last two miles of his pilgrimage, an uphill walk along winding rocky paths edged by low limestone walls.

The last turn brought him, sweating slightly, to the opening to the yard in front of his father's house. His father, whiter-haired, but as strong-looking and as straight as ever, was standing there with his back to the setting sun. He looked carefully at his returned son and stretched his arms, hands open, to their full extent.

Vincent Cullen's eyes pricked. He dropped the suitcases and the handgrip, swallowed, strode forward, and did a thing he had never before done in his life. He embraced his father.

His father stared at him irritably and said, 'Would you for God's sake get out of the way, Vincent. I'm taking the measurements of the gate.'

BILL AND COO-EE

THOSE Australians who paid any attention to such matters felt that if they must have a Pom Governor General, Field Marshal Lord Slim was as good as they'd get. The victor of the Burma campaign had an incomparable record as a fighting soldier. He was large and looked impressively tough. He had an astute mind, an earthy wit, and a facility for slipping easily from necessary formality to relaxed affability. He was genuinely interested in people. He travelled and visited tirelessly. He was fundamentally a modest man.

The wartime British press used to report that it was customary for his soldiers in the 14th Army to refer to him in their everyday conversation as 'Uncle Bill'. This, to put it at its lowest, seems inherently unlikely. But his qualities were those of the favourite uncle that most people would like to have.

In Australia he was troubled by recurrent pain from an old wound. Since he did not spare himself, and was no longer in the early bloom of youth, he became on occasion tired. When the tiredness coincided with exceptional discomfort from the wound, he sometimes fell short of being avuncular. This once became evident to a motorcycle escort.

He had flown back to Canberra from a long and exhausting tour of the Northern Territory, an expedition that he had enjoyed. He was greeted with all the formal courtesies appropriate to the Crown's representative. He acknowledged salutes, inspected, commended, shook countless hands and chatted.

Duty done, weary, wound painful, he sat back in the official car and was driven home to Government House, preceded and surrounded by an escort of motorcyclists. His immediate ambitions were limited. He wanted a drink, a bath and a rest.

When he stepped out of the car, his ADC, with the best of intentions but unwisely, suggested that a short inspection of, and a quick word with, the motorcycle escort would please them. What the ADC had in mind was a brief, uncritical stroll down the ranks, followed by a friendly, perhaps jovial, expression of thanks for their services.

The weakness in this scheme was that on the journey from the airport Slim had glanced a couple of times at the nearest motorcyclist and had been unimpressed.

What the escort got was not, therefore, cheerful old Uncle Bill, but a sudden reversion to the past when Captain W. Slim, the adjutant of the 1st/6th Gurkha Rifles, conducted the grimly alarming examinations that were the foundation of his regiment's reputation as one of the smartest in the Indian Army.

At the end of this thorough and totally silent appraisal, Slim delivered a parting message different from the one his ADC had been thinking about.

'When I looked at your uniforms I thought that you'd been cleaning your motorcycles with them. Now that I've looked at your motorcycles, I see that I was wrong.'

ON THE OTHER FOOT

THE tribulations of Captain Jenkins of Force 136 began on a moonlit March night in 1945 when he parachuted into Japanese-occupied Malaya, charged with giving training and liaison facilities to guerrillas of the Malayan People's Anti-Japanese Army.

Careful prior arrangements had been made for the jump. The selected dropping zone was a remote patch of tin-tailings, free of trees that might snag a parachute. Signals, passed through a mission dropped in earlier, had said that a reception party of guerrillas would be at the DZ to collect Jenkins, his wireless operator, and the stores that would go down in three canisters.

The RAF's navigation had been faultlessly accurate. The timing was right to within ten minutes.

The reception party was not the one that Jenkins had looked forward to meeting. The location of the dropping zone had been compromised. Japanese interlopers killed the wireless operator, confiscated the stores canisters, and fired a remarkable quantity of ammunition at Jenkins. By a freak of, from their point of view, unlucky marksmanship, they missed Jenkins himself but shot away the sole of his right jungle boot.

Jenkins sprinted for the cover of some nearby overgrown rubber, amidst rasped shouts of Nipponese frustration. There was a follow-up but it was ineffectual. Jenkins, hampered by his unshod foot, moved resolutely through the rubber until he reached its edge.

Its edge was marked by a small stream, beyond which the ground began to rise. Jenkins climbed for an hour through the primary jungle of the foothills of the main range, selected a flat patch of fern-covered earth between tall trees, sat down and considered what to do next. He soon reached the conclusion that he hadn't the remotest idea of what to do next, so he went to sleep.

When he awoke some time after dawn, he found that he was being looked at by a small, almost naked, dark man who was squatting on his hunkers and clutching a long blowpipe. Jenkins, a Malayan rubber planter in civilian life, began for the first time recently to feel at home. He liked aborigines. He said 'Good morning' in Malay.

The aborigine's Malay wasn't all that good but he had several qualities that appealed to Jenkins. Like all aborigines, he treated the jungle with cosy familiarity, a habitat full of landmarks as recognizable as street corners are to a townsman. He moved silently, blended into the background like a wraith. He was insatiably curious and he knew where everything that mattered was.

In the course of a long and friendly conversation, the aborigine said that he had watched unobtrusively the commotion at the tin-tailings on the previous night and had admired the speed of Jenkins's departure into the rubber. At dawn he had picked up Jenkins's tracks, followed them, and here he was.

He assumed that Jenkins would like to be put in touch with the white man who lived with Chinese fighters in the hidden camp on a ridge not too far away. He, the aborigine, disliked and feared the Chinese fighters, but he would gladly take Jenkins almost all the way if that was what he wanted. He would leave him to make his entry alone.

Jenkins thanked him and they set out. The aborigine's idea of not too far away differed from Jenkins's concept of distance, but shortly before dusk, and after a hairy encounter with guerrilla sentries, Jenkins was drinking tea from a tin mug with the Force 136 officer who had signalled the administrative arrangements for the disastrous drop.

This was an old peacetime friend, a former game warden. Jenkins was dismissive of his apologies and recrimination was

150

eschewed. They discussed what Jenkins, in his changed circumstances, could do to make himself useful.

It was clear that without a proper pair of boots the answer was very little. He could potter about inside the camp and do things like encoding messages and elementary weapon training, but immobilized for lack of boots he would be, he calculated, only about 25 per cent effective. As it was, his right foot was badly lacerated and swollen. Until that was put right with the help of the medical pack he wouldn't be effective at all.

The game warden said that supply drops for the guerrillas were now coming in with increasing frequency. One was due in four nights' time. He would signal Kandy to include an extra pair of jungle boots, size what? Jenkins said size ten.

Jenkins, not normally a sweet-natured man, showed exemplary patience while awaiting the drop. When it came, all canisters were retrieved and their contents distributed. Jenkins was presented with a pair of boots, size six. He continued immobile, nursing wrath.

The next resupply was ten days later. The game warden had transmitted Jenkins's dissatisfaction about the dwarf-sized boots to Ceylon and had been given an assurance that there was no possibility of the muddle over the size being repeated. It wasn't. There were no boots at all.

At this point Jenkins, patience discarded, seething with bitter rage, demanded that *he* draft the next message to Kandy. The game warden, who believed rightly that if Jenkins got at his signal traffic there would be a deterioration of relations that would prejudice the future inclusion of little personal luxuries so far fitted into spare space in the canisters, dissuaded him, with difficulty. Jenkins sulkily conceded that the game warden's 'Vital repeat vital receive boots size ten repeat size ten for Jenkins' should do the trick.

The size ten boots arrived in the next drop. They were for two left feet.

The game warden knew when he was beaten. Jenkins took over the drafting and transmission of subsequent signalled correspondence about boots.

Extract from the signal log of the message centre, Malayan Country Section, Force 136 Headquarters, Kandy

Personal from Jenkins: Will you half-witted bastards for Chrissake outfinger soonest. First you send me size six boots, then you send me no boots, then you send me two left repeat left bloody boots. It's high time you got your heads out of your arses. Do you want me to continue in this bloody war or not query.

Personal for Jenkins from Force Commander: I will not, repeat not, tolerate the use of improper and intemperate language in signals from officers in the field. Reasons are two. One, it is unmilitary and ungentlemanly. Two, cypher clerks are volunteer ladies. This sort of behaviour will get you nowhere.

Personal for Force Commander from Jenkins: Nor will two left fucking boots.

JUST HAPPENED TO BE PASSING

ONE of the few instances in which British officers were given explicit orders *not* to go into action with the troops they commanded occurred in 1949.

Fighting developed between India and Pakistan over which of them should own Kashmir. Hostilities were confined to Kashmir itself. Numbers of British officers who had formerly served in the old, undivided Indian Army were on secondment to the Indian and Pakistani forces. If these people did in its entirety the military job they were paid to do, and led their soldiers in battle, they could find themselves up against other British officers, fighting on the other side.

With the endorsement of the Indian, Pakistani and British Governments, the senior British officer in each of the combatant armies ordered that no British officer should take any part whatsoever in the Kashmir operations. Any other decision would have been indefensible. There were some recipients of the order who found it disagreeable.

Major Carr-Williams commanded a Pakistani artillery battery of 25-pounder gun-howitzers. He was a professional soldier. He loved his present job. He was devoted to his gunners. He was cheerfully uninterested in politics, regarding the role in life of the likes of him as clearing up, at the risk of his skin, the messes left by incompetent politicians. As he saw it, that role could only be fulfilled by the practice of an absolute loyalty to the soldiers he led. To be told to stay behind when they went off to fight caused him grief and anger.

He took his resentment and his copy of the order that

'YOU, DAISY PERKINS, WILL LEAD THE ATTACK, SUPPORTED BY MRS
MINIVER AND VERA LYNN'

had provoked it to the issuer of the order, Major General
Bermingham.

Their conversation was unsatisfactory.

'I can't let them go without me, sir.'

'You'll do what you're told.'

'But they're my battery. I'd never be able to face . . .'

'I know how you feel. I've been in this rather longer than
you have. This is a direct order from the top to me, and from
me to you. I don't make a practice of discussing orders, but I'll
make one comment on this one. It's entirely sensible. There's
no alternative.'

'Sir!' said Carr-Williams expressionlessly. He saluted and
left.

On the next day he waved goodbye to the soldiers he
cherished as they went off to war without him. On the day
after that he took a month's leave. He spent it in Kashmir.

*   *   *

During the second week of his leave he was sitting in his command post with a headset on, wearing a tweed suit, when a jeep bumped up the stony track behind him. For some minutes Carr-Williams neither heard nor saw it. He was concentrating upon the direction of a shoot on to a troublesome Indian position which he was fairly certain had been put where it was by an old chum named Jock, who had been in the same regiment with him in Italy.

It was only when he had temporarily stopped the shoot that he turned round and noticed that he was being observed with interest by a tall, lean European in a hacking-jacket and twill trousers.

'What are you doing here?' asked this visitor.

'Butterfly collecting,' said Carr-Williams. 'Excellent specimens in Kashmir. What about you?'

'I'm the Headmaster of Winchester visiting my Old Boys,' said General Bermingham, 'and I've just been looking at the map young Yusuf Khan here kindly lent me. If I were you, I'd shift my OP to that crest slightly to the south.'

'Yes, sir,' said Carr-Williams.

TALK OUT

GENERAL Sir Gerald Templer, who was simultaneously High Commissioner and Director of Operations for three years during the Malayan Emergency in the 1950s, was given unprecedented powers during his time in office. He used them vigorously, effectively, and with a sardonic absence of inhibition. His conversational style was crisp.

A discussion he held with an officer he met in the course of a visit to the Defence Ministry in Kuala Lumpur is illustrative. The general's appearance in this establishment was not preceded by the customary cosy notice that he would be there in a week's time, thus allowing smooth defensive preparation and the crowding of skeletons into filing cabinets. It was a surprise raid.

'What do you do?' said the general, walking lithely into an office.

'Staff Officer Plans, Nuclear Defence, sir.'

'What's your estimate of the likelihood of a nuclear strike on Malaya in the next ten years?'

'Nil.'

'I agree. You're sacked.'

SNAKES AND LADDERS

'You needn't bother much about snakes,' said the game warden reassuringly. 'You won't come across many and most of the ones you do see are harmless. But watch out for the banded krait.'

He was lecturing on junglecraft to newly arrived British troops during the Malayan Emergency. They sat in rows in loosely fitting green uniforms, looking sceptical.

'The krait is black with orange bands around it,' went on the game warden. 'There's one simple way of dealing with it. You have to be very quick. Seize it firmly by the base of the tail with both hands, hold tight with the lower hand, run the upper hand as fast as you can along it until you're grasping it just below the head. Then grip hard, keep both hands wide apart, and crack its head against a tree or a rock.'

Two weeks later the game warden went hospital visiting. He passed by the bed of a patient who peered at him gloomily from a gap in the bandages that swathed his head, face and hands. Both his arms were in plaster. A leg in traction was pointing in the air, slung from a hook in the ceiling.

'You and your bloody banded krait,' said the patient through a small space in the bandaging.

'Krait?'

'Yes, krait. I was off duty in deep jungle, and asleep. When I woke up there it was. Black with orange bands. It was swaying slowly from side to side. I did like you said – grabbed it by the end of the tail with both hands, ran the top one up fast, and *wham*.'

'Why *wham*?'

'I was holding a tiger by the arse.'

REUNION

THE introduction of computers might by now have made a difference and the contraction of British overseas commitments has certainly reduced the scope, but it was once not unknown for the War Office to post the wrong man to the wrong place at the wrong time.

An example of this occurred in 1951 during the Korean War. It became evident to a brigade headquarters that an improvement in the coordination of their arrangements with their allies would be achieved if they were to be given an additional officer, charged with looking after liaison with the South Koreans on a fulltime basis.

Realism dictated that the finding of an ideal candidate for the job, a speaker of Korean, would be unlikely. An acceptable second-best, it was suggested, would be somebody with Far Eastern experience.

The War Office found somebody with Far Eastern experience. He was an able officer who had served in Hong Kong in the late 1930s and had been captured by the Japanese in Singapore in 1942. His time as a prisoner-of-war had, of course, deprived him of the operational opportunities that had been open to luckier contemporaries. It was felt that an active appointment in Korea would help him to catch up in this respect.

He was flown out immediately. He reported himself, eager for work, at the brigade headquarters housed in a requisitioned school. The brigade major welcomed him hospitably and said that the brigade commander would see him as soon as he could. At the moment the brigadier was talking

158

to his Korean liaison officer, whose English was none too good and who was inclined to verbosity. There might be quite a wait. Have a cup of tea.

Over the tea the brigade major, who had himself drafted the job specification, put some tactful research into the newcomer's Asian background. It was impressive. Among other things he was an enthusiastic linguist who had qualified in Cantonese and Malay. He would start on Korean at once.

Had he come across any Koreans before?

Only on the railway.

The railway?

The Burma–Siam railway. Prisoners-of-war of the Japanese had been put to work building the bloody thing. It had been unpleasant. For obvious reasons, nobody at the time had been able to keep an overall count of casualties, but he'd seen the figures recently. Sixty-one thousand POWs had been sent there. Sixteen thousand had died. All the guards had been bastards. The biggest bastards of the lot had been Koreans.

The brigade major was beginning to wonder whether there might not be a touch of reserve in the new man's attitude to his allied opposite numbers, when the brigadier's door opened and the Korean liaison officer came out.

The brigade major rose to his feet to make the introductions. 'This is . . .' he started.

The newly joined member of the brigade staff drew his pistol and shot the Korean dead.

'Recognized him at once,' he explained later. 'He was one of the bastards on the railway.'

His replacement matched exactly the requirements redrafted jointly by the brigadier and the brigade major. He was a qualified Finnish speaker who had never before set foot out of Europe.

LINGUA IBANA

By the nature of things, artificial irregularities in tropical rain forest are more apparent to people who have lived in it all their lives than they are to soldiers from Western Europe with primarily urban backgrounds. Because of this self-evident truth, Iban trackers recruited in North Borneo were brought to help British infantry hunting communist terrorists during the Malayan Emergency.

The Ibans, who had tattooed faces and whose earlobes were cut into attenuated strips and then knotted, were very popular with their hosts. Their talents were valued, they fitted in well, and they laughed easily.

'But how,' asked a Malayan civil service officer of a subaltern newly returned from a patrol, 'do you communicate with them? Have you learned Iban, if that's what it's called?'

'No. We use English.'

'How much have they learned?'

'Enough. I'll give you a demonstration.'

He called the tracker's name and beckoned. The tracker joined them. The subaltern pointed to the ground, jumped about a bit, and left a compact set of jumbled footprints, pointing in several different directions. When he stopped, the tracker squatted, examined the footprints briefly and said, 'Bloody roobish.'

The subaltern moved two yards to an unsullied patch of earth and stepped carefully. This time the only imprint was of the heel of his jungle boot.

The tracker squatted again, pointed in the direction in

'HERE IS YOUR REQUEST NUMBER, SERGEANT SMART –
"THE TEDDY BEARS' PICNIC"'

which the leaver of such a trace would have been travelling,
and said, 'Not bloody roobish.'

'Quite enough for us,' said the subaltern.

BAD LANGUAGE

FOWLER was a gifted and ambitious young sapper officer with a flair for languages. In 1954 he tried, unsuccessfully, to get himself posted to Malaya.

He was unable to get there because the Army's share in a coordinated civil administration–police–military campaign was primarily a matter for infantry. The few field companies of Royal Engineers had no vacancies. He concluded that his only hope was to equip himself with some special qualification. But what? He thought deeply about various possibilities. He eliminated the doubtfuls from his mental list. He was left with one, so far an outline idea, lacking precision. It would have to be something to do with languages, his hobby and his passion.

The Malayan languages were Malay, Chinese and Tamil. His researches disclosed that the Army was well supplied with Malay speakers, that it would take two years – too long for his purposes – to reach an adequate standard in a Chinese dialect, and that Tamil was irrelevant to the Emergency.

A new development gave him something to think about. The terrorists had earlier relied for supplies and information upon thousands of rural Chinese squatters, scattered in small, isolated groups. The civil government had now resettled these into defended villages that could be properly administered. The flow of food to the Communist Terrorists, or CTs, had been heavily curtailed.

The guerrilla leadership, with many of its followers, had in consequence withdrawn to the tropical rain forest in the hills of the main range. They now extorted supplies from the aborigines, gentle people easily intimidated. Steps were being taken to help the aborigines to resist this pressure. The means chosen were patient persuasion, supplemented by the most effective hearts and minds ingredient of all, a programme of medical visiting, and the setting up of jungle forts around which aborigines could concentrate for protection when under specific threat. Trading posts for the sale or barter of aborigine produce were attached to the forts.

The Department of Aborigines looked after the persuasion, the medicine, and the trading. The Police Field Force manned the forts. The SAS operated throughout in an immense intricate area of wooded hills and valleys, seeking terrorists. The key to success was information on CT locations and habits. The police, the SAS, and the Department acted in concert in assembling and exchanging this.

Surely, thought Fowler, there could be a role here for him. If he privately learned whatever it was that aborigines spoke and then volunteered to help in the intelligence gathering and its collation, could his offer be refused? He had never so much as heard of a British military linguist fluent in Aborigine.

He consulted the School of Oriental and African Studies in London. They told him that the largest aborigine group in Malaya were the Temiar. The teaching of their language was not on the curriculum. There was no demand for it, they had no instructors in it, and since it was unwritten they could give no guidance on it. Try Cambridge. It was a long shot, but a government ethnologist named Pat Noone, who had gone into the jungle with his aborigine wife when the Japs invaded and had never been seen again, had left some fascinating monographs at Cambridge in the 1930s. There might just be something in the Noone papers, phonetic renderings perhaps, that would help Fowler.

There weren't. There was enough material though to give Fowler an absorbing day of browsing through descriptions of the lives of a simple, self-contained people, perfectly adapted to their environment, with a strong code of moral and spiritual values and a psychologically advanced mechanism for shedding fears and worries by the therapeutic open discussion of dreams. Fowler's enthusiasm for learning Temiar became an obsession.

It was a frustrating obsession. A protracted trawl could turn up no Temiar-teaching educational institution, public or private, in the United Kingdom.

Without optimism, he advertised in *The Times*. A reply came by return of post. Somebody signing himself as S. Sockalingam, who lived in Wimbledon, declared himself to be a highly accomplished language tutor, a master of Temiar, and anxious to please. Fowler went to see Mr Sockalingam.

Mr Sockalingam was a man of dignity, who said at once that he thought it proper to account for his rare seam of knowledge. For fifteen years before the war, he said, he had been a trader at Grik, in Upper Perak. Here he had met for the first time a few of the less timid Temiar, who occasionally came out of the jungle. After a period of careful cultivation, he persuaded them to barter a few blowpipes, bamboo quivers, and woven *mengkuang* back-baskets. He sent samples of these to his brother in Singapore, who sold souvenirs to travellers in visiting passenger ships. The samples were snapped up and the brother asked for more.

More blowpipes and accessories changed hands, the trade burgeoned, and Mr Sockalingam achieved a very difficult thing. Slowly, delicately, he won the Temiars' confidence. They invited him to their *ladangs* and their longhouses. He went on hunting trips with them. And he learned their language, which he would gladly teach Fowler at the reasonable fee, bearing in mind its scarcity value, of three hundred quid the course.

Fowler, who didn't have three hundred pounds, signed on, went to see his bank manager, took two weeks' leave, and started work.

It was a hideously hard language, all tones, clicks, and glottals with an eccentric grammatical form and a slaphappy absence of exactitude about time and space. The past, the present and the future were indistinguishable. There were no parallels to hours, miles or acres. But there was beauty to it, a richness in simile and allusion, a poetry in its metaphors.

Mr Sockalingam was a no-nonsense taskmaster and he kept Fowler fully stretched, at first for the daylight hours of the two-week leave period and subsequently in the evenings when Fowler drove up to Wimbledon from Aldershot. Fowler memorized words and sentence patterns, and talked and talked stumblingly, with growing confidence, with fluency. He began to think in Temiar, to dream in it.

Success came four months after a concentration of exhausting, satisfying work.

'I can do no more,' said Mr Sockalingam humbly. 'Last hundred quid, please.'

Fowler paid up, took him out to a celebratory curry, and bade him goodbye.

'You can speak what?' said Fowler's commanding officer. 'Never heard of it.'

Fowler explained. He spelt out his interest in using his unusual, so far as he knew unique, qualification in the continuing Malayan aborigine operation. At the very least, he could speed up the recording and dissemination of aborigine information. He understood that at the moment the SAS were using a mixture of elementary Malay, mime and the drawing of crude pictures with sticks in the earth.

Fowler's CO told Fowler that he would think about it. He did. He put a suggestion to the War Office. They forwarded a summary to the director of operation's staff in Kuala Lumpur. In Kuala Lumpur there was consultation between the GOC Malaya, the Aborigines Department, and the Police Field Force. Fowler was sent for.

He was flown out by RAF Transport Command. When he arrived no time was wasted. Instead of the period of briefing and acclimatization that he had vaguely expected, he was told to dump his kit in the RAF mess, was issued with jungle green equipment and a carbine, and two hours later was in a Wessex helicopter, puttering over seemingly endless tree-covered steep ridges and valleys. From above they looked like a vast, undulating field of closely planted brassicas.

He had been told the reason for the hurry. On the previous day the SAS, led by an aborigine guide, had discovered an exceptionally large CT camp. There had been a brisk fight with outlying sentries in which five CTs had been killed. The camp's occupants had dispersed in small groups, as was their invariable and tactically sensible practice on these occasions. Several simultaneous followups were in progress. There was no suggestion that Fowler, neither jungle fit nor acclimatized, should join in one of these, but it was thought that he could make himself very useful in helping to coordinate the intelligence side of the job. Fowler became irrationally happy.

The chopper put down on a cleared patch of flattened earth outside the fort. The fort was built of jungle wood, slatted bamboo, and had an *attap* roof and a small stockade. A stream ran nearby. The trading post and a few longhouses were on the fort side of the stream. All around the clearing loomed the jungle, huge bare-boled trees rising one behind the other, undergrowth shaded out by the interlocking canopy of branches high overhead. Fowler felt immediately at home. This was recognizable country, straight out of Noone's Cambridge archives.

Fowler jumped down, ducked below the rotor blade, and found himself being examined with cheerful curiosity by a crowd of half-naked, small, dark people of all ages. He shook the hand of the police lieutenant in command of the fort, and turned with assumed casualness to make his first carefully prepared witticism to real live Temiar in their own language.

It was at that point that his troubles began.

Three statements by interested parties summarized his predicament.

'Get that useless bastard out of that fort on the next chopper,' said the superintendent commanding the Police Field Force.

'He's been conned,' said the Protector of Aborigines.

'God alone knows what language he talks,' said the SAS squadron commander to his colonel. 'Whatever it is, the aborigines can't understand a bloody word of it.'

Nor, it seemed, could anybody else. Fowler, after the shortest recorded tour in military history, brought his language back to Britain. Mr Sockalingam was found to have departed prudently from Wimbledon without leaving a forwarding address. The findings of the School of Oriental and African Studies were that the Fowler tongue had a complex and in some ways sophisticated structure, which was interesting because no one in Asia or Africa spoke it. A tape recording that they asked Fowler to make was circulated among academic linguists the world over. They too liked it, but could not identify it.

Fowler, who had defied the hallowed doctrine of never volunteering for anything, has not since volunteered for anything.

TITFER TAT

U NTIL the early 1960s a convention about what civilian clothes an officer should wear whilst in London was assiduously honoured. Whether on leave, off duty, working in the War Office, or attached to another Whitehall Ministry, the accepted ensemble was a dark suit of conservative cut, a white stiff collar, a subdued tie, preferably regimental, and dark polished shoes. Essential supplements for open-air movement were a bowler hat, a rolled umbrella and gloves, the last of which on warm days could be carried in one hand, never stuffed into a coat pocket.

It was the open-air paraphernalia that bothered a young officer in the Malay Regiment. He was due for home leave in 1952 after his first three-year tour. A man of exclusively rural interests, he had intended to go straight from the troopship to his parents' home in Scotland and stay there, dressed comfortably for walking long distances over mountains and harrying fish and birds.

He had, alas, commitments in London. His colonel had entrusted him with some minor regimental business involving calls on three separate departments in the War Office. For these he was only partially equipped.

He specified his difficulty to his company commander over a drink. This London jaunt, he said, was going to be damned expensive. He was okay for the dark suit and stiff collar, although as he hadn't touched them since Sandhurst they might be a tight fit. The bowler and the umbrella were in another category altogether. He had had them too at Sandhurst, but he had deposited them in Scotland before he left for Malaya.

He could buy new ones in London, which for one-time use would be an absurd waste of money. He could go by train to Scotland and come back with the ones he'd left behind him, which would waste both money and time. Was hiring possible? Did his company commander know anything about renting bowlers and umbrellas in London?

Totally unnecessary, said his boss. The lad must use his wits. The thing to do was to lurk about in the street outside the front entrance of the War Office until nobody in a bowler was in sight. Then walk to the doorman and produce identifying pieces of paper.

The doorman would be uninterested in how any visitor was dressed. He could be wearing a stetson and suspender belt so long as he was authorized to enter. Entry was guaranteed.*

Once inside, there would be a period of polite indifference. A person in a dark suit, a stiff collar and a non-controversial tie would look like any other junior officer who had hung up his hat and umbrella and was roaming about, looking busy.

The next trick was to find the room that was to be visited. To walk in and announce the purpose of the call would be self-defeating. The thing to do was to move to the nearest hat stand in the corridors. These were overloaded with bowlers and umbrellas.

All the bowlers and all the umbrellas looked identical. A sensible caller should simply pick up the nearest of each. Then all he had to do was to carry them with him to where he was due, knock on the door, and walk in looking properly dressed.

The last phase was child's play. Say goodbye, hang up the bowler and the umbrella where they had first been found, and bugger off quick.

Practitioners of this exercise in extemporization should, of course, allow a planning margin for unexpected contingencies. The company commander had once found himself on dangerous ground when the man he had gone to see, a hospitable full colonel, had wrapped up the business part of the

---

* In the days when intruders into public buildings were nuisances, not assassins and demolition specialists.

discussion with an invitation to a mid-morning pink gin at his club. The visiting subaltern, as he then was, had no option but to walk out of the War Office with some unknown benefactor's belongings, thus being transformed instantly from a borrower into a thief.

Fortunately the hat was a reasonable fit, but any solace gained from that coincidence was offset in the club when he looked inside the bowler before hanging it up. The owner's name had been inscribed inside by the makers'. The owner was a deeply unpleasant major general whose appointment to the command of the division in which the subaltern was serving at the time had recently been announced.

A weak man might have succumbed to muddled thinking and have attempted to smuggle the hat back to its original War Office hat stand when the pink gin interlude was over. Timing was the difficulty here. There could have been an appalling uproar if the general, on his way to lunch and stopping to pick up his hat and umbrella from where he had left them, had found them being carried down a corridor towards him by the subaltern.

The subaltern took no chances. After an enjoyable drink he thanked his host, walked to the Embankment, and surprised a group of passers-by by throwing what looked like a perfectly good bowler and a perfectly good umbrella into the River Thames.

STAFF COLLEGE DRAG

F RENCH farce and Hollywood drama have it that the traditional refuge for a man in danger of being caught in bed with somebody else's wife is under the bed itself, in a wardrobe, or among the wide-open spaces beyond the window.

Major David Curtis, alerted by a bass 'Yoohoo, darling, I'm back' and the thump of baggage being grounded in the sitting room of the flat, unhesitatingly chose the window. He did this partly because it was available and open, and partly because in no circumstances did he want a confrontation with the injured party. The injured party had done two tours with the SAS and had played rugby for the army. He was short-tempered.

Curtis's initial getaway was entirely successful, but he recognized unemotionally that he was in the early stages of an intricate day. The ground-floor flat was a subdivision of an old Victorian house on Yateley Common. The garden was large and bordered by dense thickets of rhododendrons and azaleas. It was ten o'clock on a Sunday morning. Curtis, as was proper to a person being groomed for the higher reaches of his profession, took as his starting point a precise definition of his problem.

This came out as: how does a stark naked officer, sheltering on a Sunday morning in a clump of rhododendrons in a garden on Yateley Common, negotiate the two miles to his quarters in the Staff College at Camberley without attracting attention to himself?

After gloomily admiring the phrasing that he had chosen to

summarize his dilemma, Curtis examined methodically the courses open to him.

He could stay where he was until nightfall and then sneak back across country. Feasible, but it carried two disadvantages. It was early April and he would probably develop pneumonia. And that SAS hooligan might take it upon himself to do some Sunday gardening with consequent mayhem in the shrubbery.

Break into a house and steal some clothes? Too risky. A conviction for nude burglary would do his career no good.

Steal a car? Same objection.

Telephone a friend for help? Naked men in public call boxes invite comment and anyhow his money was in the pocket of the trousers that he hoped Marcia had had the wit to hide successfully.

He was becoming progressively colder as he weighed these considerations. His teeth chattered. Clearly he must move soon. Where to?

Well, somewhere closer to the Staff College for a start. Why not make his way cautiously across the half mile or so of Yateley Common that separated him from the A30 and lie up somewhere near the main road? He could then exploit any chance opportunities that came up, although he was unable to imagine what they might be.

He broke carefully from cover, crossed a gravelly track, and headed over the common. The common was prolific in heather and bracken and scrubby clusters of birch and brambles. To anyone taking no chances and reasonably knowledgeable in fieldcraft, it was easy to evade morning dog walkers, occasional church-goers, and talkative children with model boats on their way to play at the pond.

He selected as his first hiding-up place a clump of broom. It lay beside a footpath that ran up a shallow embankment to the verge of the A30. Here he examined the multiple lacerations slashed by gorse and brambles. They were painful but not too bad. The same with the big toe that he had stubbed on a stone.

It was time to ponder on his next move. The pondering did not prosper. About the only thing he could think of was to try to jump a truck. But for this to be profitable would demand an unlikely conjunction of happenings. A slowed truck, a driver looking elsewhere, no observers, and the truck going to the right place, which would be one of the lonely lanes near Sandhurst. If all that fell into place, and if. . . . But what was this? He was conscious of a persistent, dull, drumming sound, interspersed with heavy breathing, coming from the direction of the path, coming closer.

He peered cautiously through the foliage. Jogging towards him was a sweating, preoccupied, plump man, dressed in singlet and shorts, breathing stertorously. Behind this fat athlete was a succession of others of differing sizes, seemingly hundreds of them, stretching away as far as the eye could see. Some wore singlets, some windcheaters, some were stripped to the waist. All looked intensely introspective, concentrating on aching leg muscles and distended lungs.

This was it. Curtis picked a small gap in the line, moved unobtrusively from cover, and joined in the exertions of enthusiasts getting themselves into shape for the London Marathon.

He was pleased to find that not only could he jog among them in comfortable, unremarked anonymity but that they were going in the right direction. They scrambled up the bank to the A30 in single file, turned left, and ran towards Camberley, the Staff College, and sanctuary.

Once on the road the single file became ragged. Runners coalesced into small, panting groups. Curtis tucked his nudity thankfully into the middle of one of the groups and began to work out how to disengage himself when he reached the Staff College gates. Nothing much to it. A quick short sprint to the guardroom, some jokey lies about how his shorts were ripped to uselessness by brambles, a telephone call to the mess, and he would be home and dry.

A healthy looking runner whose breathing was better than most trotted up beside Curtis and became inquisitive.

'Excuse me,' he said, 'I'm something of a student of running techniques. Do you always run in the nude?'

Curtis considered it. He'd better do something to placate

this nut. Otherwise the fellow, presumably some sort of official or coach, might make later embarrassing inquiries about the identity of the demon starko strider.

'Yes,' said Curtis, panting, 'cuts down wind resistance. Also exposure of the maximum skin surface stimulates blood flow.'

'Thanks,' said the inquirer, dropping away astern.

They were surging through Blackwater when Curtis became aware once more of a presence at his shoulder.

'Excuse me,' said the inquisitive voice, this time puffing noticeably. 'I see that you're running in bare feet. Do you always run in bare feet?'

'Yes,' panted Curtis, 'if you get the soles hardened, it's fine. The total energy saved over long distances by not having to carry the weight of shoes, however light, is enormous.'

'Thanks,' said the student of technique. He dropped away again. He was back, infuriatingly, as the Staff College gates approached.

'Excuse me,' he panted.

'Yes?'

'Do you always wear a contraceptive when you run?'

'No,' called Curtis as he began his sprint for the guard-room, 'but it was raining this morning when I left home.'

JUST IN CASE

ONE of the more unpleasant tropical diseases is a liver ailment known as sprue. Its victims become fevered, debilitated, and can die if not given correct medical treatment.

The RAMC medical orderly with a detached company of the Durham Light Infantry, training in remote country in central India, diagnosed three instances of this malady. He reported his findings to the company commander and urged immediate evacuation of the patients to hospital.

The company commander, who had never before heard of sprue, was hesitant. He had his training cycle to complete. He wanted to put as many people through it as possible. He respected the medical orderly's competence in dealing with day-to-day cuts, sprains and disordered stomachs, but was less sanguine about his knowledge of exotic complaints of which he himself was ignorant. He decided to ask for a second opinion on whether evacuation would really be necessary.

His communications to his battalion headquarters were by an elderly wireless set that transmitted in Morse. By education and habit the company commander wasted no words on the air.

At the end of his daily message, in which he summarized training progress and listed his supply requirements, he added, 'Three cases of sprue here. Advise on disposal.'

The reply came from the orderly officer, a young man who had been enjoined continually not to bother his betters with trivia.

175

'Your para 5. Suggest the Seaforth's sergeants' mess. They'll drink anything.'

'DON'T ARGUE WITH THE COLONEL! IF THE COMPUTER SAYS YOU'RE A WRAC, YOU'RE A WRAC – AND YOU'RE IMPROPERLY DRESSED!'